D1276563

CLEON

CLEON

by **CLEON JONES**
with **Ed Hershey**

Coward-McCann, Inc.
New York

Copyright © 1970 by Cleon Jones and Ed Hershey

All rights reserved. This book, or parts thereof, may not be reproduced in any form without permission in writing from the publisher. Published on the same day in Canada by Longmans Canada Limited, Toronto.

A Maddick Manuscripts Book

Library of Congress Catalog Card Number: 78-113524

PRINTED IN THE UNITED STATES OF AMERICA

For four women behind the man
—Mama Myrt, Mrs. McCants, Angela, and Anja

40311

Contents

Editor's Note

For seven years, from their first season in 1962 through 1968, the New York Mets were a joke, and nothing about them was funnier than their hitting. Twice—in 1967 with Tom Seaver and in 1968 with Jerry Koosman—the Mets came up with an obviously gifted pitcher, but they never found anyone more than faintly resembling a hitter. One year their leading hitter batted only .253. A hitting streak for a Met looked like a slump for anyone else. Their lineup did more to reduce earned-run averages than anything since the dead ball.

But in 1969 the joke ended. The Mets became winners, and, not coincidentally, they finally produced a genuine batting star, a twenty-seven-year-old outfielder from Mobile, Alabama, named Cleon Joseph Jones.

Cleon Jones batted .340 in 1969, the third highest average in the major leagues. Statistically, Cleon batted 34 points higher than any Met had ever hit before; actually, Cleon's edge over any previous Met was far greater. In earlier years opposing teams tried not to waste their best pitchers against the Mets; in 1969 the Mets faced the best almost all the time. In earlier years opposing pitchers did not have to bear down on the Mets; in 1969 the Mets put pressure on everyone.

Cleon Jones' .340 was a solid .340, built on line drives and hard-hit ground balls, a thoroughly professional performance by a thoroughly professional ballplayer. He firmly established himself as the latest in the long line of black baseball heroes who had emerged from Mobile, starting with Satchel Paige and running through Hank Aaron, Billy Williams, and Willie McCovey to Jones' New York Met teammate, Tommie Agee.

A week after the Mets won the 1969 World Series, Mobile held a Baseball Day parade to honor a group of its white and black major-leaguers. Three bands, half a dozen city and state officials, and five thousand citizens, most of them black, turned out for the parade. Cleon Jones and Tommie Agee were the stars of the day.

In the middle of the parade Agee turned to Jones. "It feels a lot better," Tommie said, "to be riding up the street with the cops in *front* of us."

A few days later Cleon sat in the living room of the house in which he had been raised and talked about what it was like to grow up in Plateau, one of the black sections of Mobile. Cleon is a quiet man who prefers to keep his emotions within himself; he usually enjoys what he is doing and does what he enjoys. He is not a complainer. "You know," he said, shaking his head, "I really don't know how I made it. I don't know how any of us made it."

It was no surprise that white Mobile virtually ignored the parade that honored Cleon Jones and Tommie Agee. Officially, Plateau is a part of the incorporated city of Mobile, but in the minds of both the white citizens and the black, Plateau is a world apart.

During the World Series the local paper, the Mobile *Press Register,* paid scant attention to baseball, concentrating instead on the local religion, daily interviews with coach Bear Bryant on the progress of the University of Alabama's all-white football team. Each day, as the Mets played the Baltimore Orioles, the New York *Daily News* mailed a bundle of its papers to Mobile County High School so that the students could follow in detail the feats of the school's former students Cleon Jones and Tommie Agee.

When I traveled to Mobile to work with Cleon on his story, I called the Mobile *Press Register* and asked for permission to examine its file on Cleon Jones. "I'd like to check the statistics on his high school baseball and football games," I said.

The man who answered the phone asked me to wait a minute.

Then he came back on the line. "I'm sorry," he said, "but we don't have a Cleon Jones file."

Nothing can tell you more about Cleon's background. This book is simply to fill in the gaps.

New York City   Ed Hershey
February, 1970

CLEON

1

Tell the Fish They'd Better Hide

"Come on, sucker, hit it to me," I said to myself.

I have to believe that eight other guys in New York Met uniforms were thinking the same thing at the same time. There was a time when every Met in the field prayed that each ball would be hit to someone else, but those days were dead.

Now it was the ninth inning of the fifth game of the 1969 World Series, and Davy Johnson, the second baseman of the Baltimore Orioles, was coming to bat. Boog Powell of Baltimore was standing on first base, and two men were out. We were in front 5–3. One more out, and we would win our fourth straight over the Orioles. One more out, and we would be the champions of the whole world.

"Come on, sucker, hit it to me."

Automatically, I reviewed our scouting report on Johnson— "Throw him good stuff and jam him"—and even though he'd had only one single in fifteen times at bat in the World Series, even though I knew he was basically a singles hitter, I moved back a few steps deeper than usual. "If he hits one over the left-field wall," I thought, "it better be more than a foot or two over. 'Cause if it ain't, I'm gonna catch the ball."

I looked over to center field, and I saw that Tommie Agee was playing a step or two deeper than normal, too. Tommie and I usually think alike, maybe because we grew up together in Mobile, Alabama, and played baseball and football together in high school.

Jerry Koosman pitched, and Davy Johnson swung.

He connected.

The crack of the bat gave me the first hint the fly ball was coming my way. I watched the ball rise above the five tiers of Shea Stadium, each painted a different color, and even before I could spot the ball outlined against the sky, I began drifting toward left-center field. I knew already, from the ball's arc and speed, from experience, where it would be coming down. I knew it would be playable.

The sucker had hit it to me. Tommie Agee had made two of the greatest catches in the history of the World Series in the third game, and Ron Swoboda had made a sensational diving catch in the fourth game. But this one was going to be mine, and this one was the sweetest because it meant the final out of the final game.

"Come on down, baby," I kept saying. "Come on down."

I caught the ball, touched my left knee to the ground in a bit of a bow, then picked myself up and took off for the Mets' bullpen in right-center field. With Johnson's fly ball still in my glove, I followed Agee through the bullpen gate and along the ramp under the stands leading to the Mets' dressing room. By the time Tommie and I arrived, the party had already begun. The champagne had already started to flow. I sprayed my share of champagne and drank my share of beer—it tastes better than champagne to me—and then I got dressed and went to my apartment in the Jamaica section of Queens to see my wife and daughter and some friends of ours who had come to New York for the Series.

I sat there in our apartment, a can of beer in my hand and our four-year-old daughter, Anja, on my lap, just trying to enjoy what had happened. Somebody called to tell us there would be a parade in New York and some other receptions for the Mets. But I'd had enough of that kind of excitement. We'd become the best in baseball that afternoon. I understood that we were sharing it with the people of New York; that was fine. But I also wanted to share it with my family and friends.

I was a star. I'd hit .340, to finish third in the National League batting race, and we had won the National League pennant and the World Series. I could have whatever I wanted. And now all I wanted was to return to Mobile and my old neighborhood, Plateau, to the people I grew up with, the people who knew me and helped me when I had nothing.

One of those I wanted most to share my victory with was my grandmother.

The phone hadn't rung twice in the little house on Edwards Street in Plateau when my grandmother answered and said, "Cleon?"

We'd bought her a color television the week before, and she'd seen all the games. But I think she would've just as soon been out on one of the creeks fishing.

"Mama Myrt," I told her. "I'm coming home. Tell the fish they'd better hide."

2

Long Walks over Short Distances

It wasn't until I went off to college and was away for weeks and months at a time that I realized the most noticeable thing about Plateau was the smell.

Two paper mills tower over the neighborhood, turning pulp into tissues and towels and bags twenty-four hours a day, seven days a week. The mills have been good for Mobile and good for Plateau, which is on the northeast side of town. As usual, the mills have been better for the whites; they get the cleaner, higher-paying jobs, and they live far enough away to avoid the smell unless the wind's blowing their way.

There isn't a section of Mobile that can totally escape the smell of the mills. But in Plateau we're close enough to get it no matter which way the wind blows. It's sort of a sticky, sweet odor that makes the air seem heavy. I guess if you grow up with something, you get used to it. But I've been told that the smell of Plateau was once used as evidence in court. A civil-rights lawyer who was fighting one of the integration cases bottled the air and presented it as evidence that no child who was forced to spend his whole life breathing and smelling that stuff could be living as the equal of a child who didn't.

Aside from the smell, two things set Plateau apart: how it looks and how it acts. An outsider would see the little shacks, some of them on streets that are not paved, and think immediately that it's a poor neighborhood. For the most part it is. But more than that, it's a rural neighborhood. There are still chickens in many of the yards, and people still go into their gardens to pick some of their dinner. I can go blocks before I see someone I don't know, and I can take long walks over short distances, because there is always something to say to everyone I see.

The people make themselves available. I didn't think there was anything special about that until I moved to New York. During the season, my wife and I live on the twelfth floor of an apartment house that probably has half as many people living in it as all of Plateau. But we can go days without seeing another person who lives in the building. And if we do see someone, the chances are it's while going up or down in the elevator, and each of us is trying very hard to pretend the other's not there. New Yorkers have a habit of looking right through each other.

The poverty in Plateau is different from the city's. Some of the people may be just as poor, or even poorer, in dollars and cents, but they have more pride down there, and, maybe because they don't get a chance to see wealth so much, they seem more willing to accept life.

I don't mean to say that they don't aspire to something better. They do. And judging from the kids who grew up with me, I would guess that the percentage of guys who have walked out of the poverty in Plateau in the last generation is greater than those who have gotten out of the city ghettos. It is just that while most of the people of Plateau want something better, they're still grateful for what they have. They know what they've lived through, and it's given them a feeling of strength and togetherness. A feeling of soul. Up North these days, soul is an "in" word, but it doesn't have the meaning that it has down in Plateau. I have to laugh when I see some wealthy blacks who've lived on steak all their lives pretending they enjoy hamhocks and chitterlings—soul food—to prove they're with it. I love hamhocks and chitterlings because I was raised on them, but I wouldn't blame my little girl for liking steak and lamb chops better.

Plateau's soul goes a lot deeper than food or music or clothes. They say now that the study of black history will give our kids more pride in being black. Down in Plateau we're one step ahead of the game because we've lived black history and we already have that pride. It never put food on our table or clothes on our backs, and it didn't make us run any faster when the white kids came by in cars and threw rocks at us. But it did keep us together.

They didn't teach the kids black history in our black schools in Plateau. They didn't have to. The man who owns most of Plateau today is Augustus Meaher, the grandson of Timothy Meagher, who in 1859 brought the last shipload of slaves from Africa to the United States. These slaves were the people who originally settled Plateau.

When I was a little boy, I knew a man named Cudjoe Lewis, who had come across from Africa on that last slave ship. Cudjoe must've been more than a hundred when he died in the early 1950's, but he liked to tell stories of his childhood in Africa and the trip to America. From listening to him and from some research a friend of mine did for a college course, I learned a little about the history of the neighborhood I grew up in.

Old Cudjoe said that all the slaves on Meagher's ship, the *Clotilde,* came from a tribe in West Africa called the Tarkars, a peaceful band of farmers who lived in mud huts, raised animals, and grew crops. The way Cudjoe described the Tarkars, they sounded a lot more civilized than some Americans. He said there was absolutely no stealing in the Tarkar village; a man could leave his purse near the marketplace and come back days later to find it undisturbed. He said, too, that each Tarkar man could have three wives, and the way the system worked seems pretty logical. A man's first wife was expected to work as long and hard as her husband, but she stopped working once her husband took a second wife. The new wife became the worker. So naturally, the first wife recruited the second wife, the second recruited the third, and everyone was happy. Except maybe the third wife. She really had it tough. Three was the limit, and I guess the better ones got drafted in the early rounds.

The Tarkars lived pretty happily, about 100 miles inland in West Africa, in one of the most fertile regions in the world. They had their own religion, with a heaven and a hell and a belief in man's soul. They didn't have temples of worship because they felt the world was their church. A good crop was a sign from heaven, from *Ala-ara.* Thunder and lightning were signs of evil, direct from hell, *Ala-bady-oleelay.*

There probably never would have been a Plateau in Mobile if another West African tribe, the Dahomeyans, hadn't been jealous of the Tarkars' prosperity. The Dahomeyans lived closer to the coast in a less fertile region, and while the Tarkars raised their children to be farmers, the Dahomeyans raised theirs to be warriors.

One day early in 1859, Cudjoe told me, a scouting party from Dahomey went to the Tarkars and demanded half their crops and livestock. The Tarkars refused. A few weeks later the Dahomeyans returned with a full army, overwhelmed the Tarkars, and beheaded the very young and the very old. Only the strongest Tarkars were allowed to live, and they were chained together and marched by the Dahomeyans to the West African coast.

After three weeks in a stockade the Tarkars were sold by the Dahomeyans to Captain William Foster, the master of the *Clotilde,* Timothy Meagher's slave ship. Augustus Meaher—the family eventually dropped the "g" from the name—told a friend of mine that the slaves were purchased for $10 apiece, but an old book my friend found said that strong slaves were so rare by 1859 that Foster paid $8,640 in gold, ninety cases of rum, and eight cases of cloth for one hundred and seventy-five Tarkars.

The *Clotilde* was humane compared to other slave ships. It was big—327 tons displacement—and its hold was large enough for the captives to move around a little. It wasn't that Timothy Meagher was out to win the Slavemaster of the Year award when he built the ship. It was just that he didn't want the *Clotilde* to look too obviously like a slave ship. He was playing an illegal game.

The importing of slaves had been outlawed in 1803, but by 1859 the Civil War was about to begin, and Meagher, confident that the South would win, wanted to get a head start on the new slave market.

Once the ship sailed across the Atlantic, into the Gulf of Mexico and up through the Mississippi Sound toward Mobile, Meagher took fantastic precautions not to get caught by federal troops with the slaves. He had a tugboat guide the *Clotilde* into

Mobile Bay, dodging bayous, marshes, and islands, then up the Spanish River to meet a steamboat. The slaves were transferred to the steamboat, and the *Clotilde* was burned, destroying one piece of evidence of Meagher's illegal activities. The steamboat brought the slaves to an old plantation more than 30 miles north of Mobile. In the next few weeks and months, as suspicious federal troops searched unsuccessfully for the slaves and Meagher was tried for slave trading and found not guilty (for lack of evidence), the Tarkars were shifted from one plantation to another, hidden in the woods and in barns.

When the pressure from federal troops subsided, Meagher managed to sell off twenty-five of the slaves and moved the rest to his plantation outside Mobile. The Tarkars soon set up their own community in a cluster of huts at the mouth of Chickasabogue Creek on a mound shaded by oak trees. It looked more like home than any other place they could find.

Freed after the Civil War, the Tarkars continued to work for Meagher, paying him rent, barely managing to scrape out a living. Their goal was to save enough money to return to Africa, but it was an impossible dream. Instead, their daily lives on what had been Meagher's plantation, in the place the Tarkars called Plateau, made them more and more a part of America. They were converted to Christianity by other blacks, and they stayed together, building cabins on the land they rented from Meagher.

They even married among themselves. Cudjoe Lewis—he got his name from his slave owner—married a Tarkar girl, and their descendants still live only a couple of blocks from my grandmother's house on Edwards Street.

Gus Meaher, Timothy's grandson, still collects rent from most of the people in Plateau, and when my friend went to talk to him about Plateau, he said we were "good nigrahs." Gus Meaher and the other white people are starting to meet some "bad nigrahs" these days, younger people who would like to have some of the better jobs at the paper mills or go to some of the better schools in town.

Actually, the Meaghers were pretty big losers on us. Before

he died, old Tim once figured out that the last slave ship to land in America lost him more than $100,000. That just breaks me up, you know. I wonder how he would feel if he knew that part of his $100,000 wound up helping the New York Mets win a World Series.

3

I Never Hated a White Man

There were three generations of my mother's family living in two houses at the corner of Edwards and Shelby streets when I was born. My great-grandmother and grandmother lived in one house on the corner lot, my mother and father in the other. I was born, as my brother, Tommie Lee, had been two years before, right in the house, delivered by the local midwife. Lots of kids were born in hospitals by that time, the summer of 1942, but my mother preferred to have her children at home.

My father was a truck driver, but at times there wasn't a whole lot of work available. The plants and factories hadn't come to Mobile yet, and even during World War II most black men who weren't glorified slaves to the few remaining wealthy whites didn't have jobs at all. Vegetables were grown, barnyard animals were raised, and fish were caught, but that could be a woman's work. There was very little to keep a man going in Plateau or the whole Mobile area if he happened to be black. And a lot of black men left in search of employment up North, in the cities. When I was three years old, my father, Joseph Jones, left for Chicago. But he didn't exactly head North willingly.

My parents had gone downtown one day, and they were going to take the bus back to Plateau. My mother was on line waiting for the bus, and behind her there was a white woman. Now this was during World War II, a long time before anyone ever heard of the Black Revolution. Blacks were supposed to go to the back of the bus. We did. But this was just the line of people waiting to get on the bus. There were no rules about *that*. Still, there was a white man nearby who decided he would make one. He told my mother, "Hey, nigger, don't go standing in front of no white woman."

My mother either didn't hear him or pretended she didn't. She just stood there. She had long hair then, and she wore it in a ponytail. The white man walked up behind her and yanked it. "Hey, nigger," he said again, "didn't you hear me tell you not to stand in front of a white lady?"

My father hadn't said anything up until then. A black man, he had learned to take a lot. But when he saw that guy pull my mother's hair, it was just too much. He didn't kill the white man, but he beat on him pretty good. That was when my father left Mobile. I guess, technically, he was running from a fugitive warrant for his arrest, if not from someone with a bullwhip. In any event, he didn't stay around long enough to find out.

So a couple of visits that my brother and I took to Chicago and a couple of trips back down that my father took years later were all Tommie Lee and I saw of him through our childhood.

My father, who sees me play almost every time I'm in Chicago now, was a pretty fair baseball player, I'm told. I know he played semipro with Satchel Paige, who was born and raised in Mobile. But of course when my father was young, there wasn't much in the game for black players. Paige was the greatest, right up there in ability with Christy Mathewson and Walter Johnson. But until Bill Veeck gave him a chance to pitch in the majors when he was already past forty, Paige barely scratched out his meal money barnstorming from town to town in broken-down old cars and rickety old buses.

For all the hard times we had, I guess all of us who grew up in Mobile in my generation—starting with Hank Aaron and going through Willie McCovey, Hank's brother, Tommie Aaron, Billy Williams, Tommie Agee, myself, and Amos Otis— were lucky to be born when we were. I mean without the opportunity to play ball, and more important, without the knowledge that there was an opportunity, I might have ended up in a lot worse shape than my father did. I never ran from a fight in my

life, and I guess I've started a few. And if I'd had nothing more
to look forward to than hustling some dinner money in Mobile,
I could have had some serious problems.

My mother left two years after my father did. She went to
Philadelphia—she had an aunt there—to find work. I guess she
planned to come back in a short time, but she never made it.
My grandmother talked about her a lot, and Tommie Lee and I
spoke to her on the phone, but aside from that, I never really
knew my mother after I was five years old.

I mentioned that there were two houses on that 102-by-102-
foot lot on Edwards Street. My great-grandmother remained in
the larger one, and my grandmother raised my brother and me
in the smaller house. My grandmother's name is Myrtle, and
we called her "Mama Myrt." I do to this day. She was the only
mother I ever really knew. Even though it was a struggle for her
trying to keep the three of us going, she saw to it that Tommie
Lee and I got the things we needed. She was a cook at Mobile
County Training High School, and she didn't make much
money. But if one of the three of us went without something,
it was usually Mama Myrt.

She sacrificed everything. Everything was always for us, always
to try to keep the two boys going. She did have a dream, though
—a dream of the day my mother would come back to us. Then,
suddenly, she didn't even have that.

The telegram telling us that my mother was dead came in the
middle of the night. My grandmother read it and then started
screaming, "My baby's dead. Oh, my daughter, my only daughter."

I was in the fifth grade then. My brother and I were awakened
by the screams. We got up and walked out on the porch. Mama
Myrt was sitting there crying, saying over and over, "Your
mother's dead."

I guess Tommie Lee and I started crying, too. But when my
grandmother looked at us and sobbed, "My poor babies, you
have no one now," we knew she was wrong. We had Mama Myrt.

Today, so far as I'm concerned, my grandmother *is* my
mother. I believe quite a few people down in Mobile, people
who don't know us very well, think to this day that Mama Myrt

is our natural mother and not our grandmother. She certainly looks young enough, despite her age—she's sixty-four—and all the years of hard work.

Mama Myrt, whose first husband was named Henson, later married a man who, coincidentally, is named Jones, John Jones. And occasionally that adds to people's confusion. After we'd won the 1969 World Series and I'd come home to Plateau, John Jones was walking with a friend in Mobile one night and was shot in the arm, accidentally, we think, by a sniper. The wire services carried the story from coast to coast: My father had been shot. Actually, it was my step-grandfather.

My father, who works for a Chicago packinghouse, was perfectly well. Imagine what Joe Jones thought when he picked up the paper the next day and read that he'd been hit in the arm by a bullet a thousand miles away.

I got into quite a bit of trouble as a kid, mischief mostly. But Mama Myrt was like any mother. She never thought there was any badness in her kids. She was just a very kind, wonderful woman who, deep down, expected everyone else to be that way, too.

I was more outgoing than my brother, and I was always the type of kid who didn't believe what someone would tell me. You had to *prove* it to Cleon. If you said I couldn't jump off a building and I said I could, I would go up to the roof and jump. Luckily, Plateau didn't have any tall buildings.

I always wanted to be the best at whatever I did. In football, for example, if somebody tackled me hard, or if I couldn't move the ball, I'd get real angry. And I was fortunate to have the physical equipment to back up my temperament. But there were some fistfights and some long walks home.

There were guys who had a little more than I had—gloves, bats, balls, and things like that. When they got angry, they could pick up their stuff and go home and stop the game. I wasn't that fortunate. If I got angry and wanted to quit, I went home the way I'd come—with nothing.

In baseball, I played the infield as a kid—shortstop and third base—and I pitched some. I loved shortstop—that's right, I was a left-handed shortstop. We had a softball team in the fifth grade at the Whitley School, which was just down the block from our house. Our teacher, Mrs. Howard, was the coach, and she knew something about baseball but not enough to know that left-handers aren't supposed to play short or third.

Usually we played ball on the street or on vacant lots. There was none of this Little League or Babe Ruth League stuff for us in Plateau, and as a matter of fact, we didn't always play ball with a ball. We improvised with anything that resembled one. Once you got involved in a game, it didn't matter that much, so long as you were playing something and trying to win.

Sports were everything. I wasn't the type of kid who really liked movies or dancing or things like that. I was always sports-minded, and I always wanted to play, not watch.

My brother would go to County High games, but I would rather throw a ball around than watch the older kids play. I didn't go to any of the high school football games, except maybe the big Thanksgiving Day game against Central High, County's big rival.

I did listen to baseball games on the radio, though, but then, I'd always be doing something else at the same time. As for television, I can remember only two television sets in all of Plateau, so if we were lucky, we might see a World Series game or a big football game on TV.

I didn't own my first baseball glove until I was thirteen years old. I remember the day I bought it. My father had come down from Chicago to visit us, and he gave Tommie Lee and me money for gloves. We took the bus downtown to the sporting goods store. First my brother bought his. We had fifteen dollars between us, and his glove cost about nine dollars. I walked around the store, trying to find one I liked. Finally I found the glove I wanted, but we didn't have enough money left for it.

I gave the man all we had—I still owed him thirty or forty cents—and Tommie Lee and I didn't have any money for the bus ride home. So we walked, out Telegraph Road and over the bridge to Plateau, a good three or four miles. We didn't notice the distance. With no ball, we picked up rocks and played catch all the way home. I just kept looking down at my new glove and pounding my fist into it. It was the most pleasant walk I think I've ever taken.

About three or four blocks from Plateau was another black area, called Magazine Point. Plateau and Magazine Point were natural rivals. We had a team that we called the Plateau Bumblebees. It was just a name we'd picked from somewhere. They called their team the Magazine Baby Bears because the Magazine sandlot team, for the older guys, was called the Bears. We played Magazine Point on Sundays. If we weren't playing Magazine Point, we were over at Happy Hill, which was about a fifteen-minute walk, playing their team.

On weekdays after school we were in the streets playing stickball or canball. Canball, now there was a game. We'd get Pet or Carnation milk cans and a broomstick. It was a soft-pitch game (no brushbacks allowed), and I guess I was the Babe Ruth of my canball league.

When we weren't playing canball, we were playing tops. We got a bunch of soda-pop tops and played pretty much the same game, trying to hit them with a broomstick, except that you could pitch the tops in as fast as you wanted to and make them curve if you could. That was a pretty good game for helping to develop hitters, so long as the tops stayed out of their eyes. You had to concentrate up there.

Canball was more my type of game than tops was. There were guys on the block who hit the pop tops a lot more often than I did. It was more of a game for the smaller guys, like our shortstop on the Mets, Bud Harrelson. Bud would've been a tops star. Fellows with short, contact-type swings had a better shot. It wasn't until years later, after I was in pro ball, that I realized you could go both ways as a hitter, big swing and little swing. But I think games like canball and tops helped develop my coordination.

When we were lucky enough to have a real baseball, we wouldn't "waste" it on weekdays. We'd save it for the Sunday games, and when we got one, it was only because we'd gone out and scraped up some money shining shoes. We opened a shoe-shine stand right on my corner, the corner of Edwards and Shelby. People would come by on the way to church on Sunday mornings, and we'd shine their shoes. Or we'd go to their houses maybe six or seven o'clock in the morning, pick up their shoes, shine them, and return them to their doorsteps before they were ready to leave for church. We charged fifteen cents a shine, and by about ten o'clock we'd have enough money to buy a ball.

Some of us had to go to church ourselves, so we always started the games at two o'clock.

We had a platoon system for our shoe-shining operation. The Catholic kids would go to church early in the morning, while the rest of us manned the stand. Then they'd come back, change, and take over so we Baptists and Methodists could go to church. Then we could all play ball.

We'd play our games in vacant lots. We'd dig trenches for base lines, put a little dirt where we knew the mound was supposed to be, find something to carve a home plate out of, and that was it—instant baseball field. Wherever we played, right field was always shorter than left field. The lots were rectangular, so one side had to be short, and since most guys are right-handed, we made left field, where they'd hit most of their shots, the long field.

But I was a left-handed hitter. I've done everything left-handed for as long as I could remember. Everything but hit a baseball, that is. I became a right-handed hitter because of Best Street.

Best Street was a block in Plateau that we used for our street games. There was a tree that made a perfect home plate and served as a backstop, too, so we wouldn't have to chase a ball that got by the catcher. But the tree, of course, was not in the middle of the roadway. It was on one side. That meant that left field ran as long as the street did, but right field would go only to the other side.

Batting left-handed I would hit the ball through somebody's window or, worse than that, into a vacant lot across the street that was filled with trash. If you lost the ball, you stopped the game. I never wanted to be the one who lost the ball. So Best Street made me a right-handed hitter.

I didn't mind because at the time Mickey Mantle was just

becoming a star, and I knew he was a switch-hitter. So in our Sunday games I began to switch-hit, right-handed against left-handed pitchers, left-handed against righties. The idea, I knew, was that you could see the pitcher release the ball better if you were standing on the side opposite his pitching arm.

In junior high school I started hitting right-handed all the way, and I just never thought about it after that. I felt more comfortable on the right side for some reason. There were three or four other guys in the neighborhood who did the same thing —throw left and hit right—so it seemed pretty normal to me. It wasn't until I entered organized baseball that I found out it was peculiar.

There are a lot of infielders who do it the opposite way. They throw right-handed because it would be awkward to fire a grounder to the first baseman as a lefty, and they hit from the left side because infielders are usually fast, and they can get an extra two steps to first starting from the left-hander's side of home plate.

I had a similar quirk in football. I threw left-handed and kicked with my right foot. But except for hitting, kicking and holding a fishing rod, I still do everything left-handed, including signing contracts, which is the most important thing a ball-player does after hitting and throwing.

The first TV set in Plateau belonged to a man named Nelse Adams, who lived a couple of blocks from me. He had a big house, and kids from all over the neighborhood would be hanging out of the windows watching the TV. The second one was bought by a lady named Mary Jackson, who ran a store that was even closer. She had the set up on an icebox in her store, and all the kids would hang around there. But Mobile wasn't a major-league town, and back then the only baseball that the local stations carried was the World Series and All-Star games, so the closest I got to knowing what was happening in the majors was when I listened to games on the radio.

It was the same thing with boxing. I was a tremendous boxing fan when I was young, but I never saw the champions fight. As a kid I boxed at the local gym. I was pretty good. I'd always been strong, and with a little coaching I got to the point where there was nobody in my rank who could handle me. That's what ended my boxing career. One day the guy who ran the gym put me in the ring with an older fellow. He hit me once and I quit right then, right that night, in the ring. I went home and never got into the ring again. My grandmother didn't want me to box, anyway, but there were other things my grandmother didn't want me to do that I did.

One of them was play football. I liked to run and I liked to hit, so it was only natural that I'd play football for County High. Besides, in Plateau everyone played everything. In junior high and before that, we always imitated the high school kids. If it was basketball season, we played basketball. If it was spring, we played baseball. And in the fall, on the streets and in the vacant lots, we had our own brand of football.

But Mama Myrt made it plain she didn't want me playing high school football, and I told her I wouldn't. I think I really meant it when I said it, too, but all the guys I'd grown up with went out for the team when we were freshmen. After a few days of standing around the field watching practice, I told the coach, Charles Rhodes, that I wanted to play. He gave me a uniform, and suddenly I was a football player.

Once I had the jersey on my back, I guess my grandmother didn't have much of a choice. Still, I didn't say anything at home until I had to get permission papers signed for insurance. My brother was also out for the team that year, and I guess that helped persuade Mama Myrt. I told her not to worry because they gave you equipment to protect you. At the time, I didn't know much about the equipment. Before I started practicing at County, I'd never even tried on a pair of cleats.

I have a good reason to remember the first jersey Mr. Rhodes handed me, in August, 1957. It was a red one, the kind that the scrubs wore when they scrimmaged against the varsity, and it almost ended my football career only a few days after it started.

We were in a scrimmage, and I was playing safety for the red-shirts, the scrubs. The varsity quarterback threw a pass, and I intercepted it and started running the ball back upfield. I always had pretty good speed, and there I was, a freshman intercepting a pass against the varsity. I was running down the sidelines when I saw another guy in a red shirt coming up alongside me. I figured I'd picked up a blocker. I was wrong. The guy's name was Turner, and he was no blocker.

He was a varsity lineman who'd torn his jersey a few minutes earlier. Instead of sending him back to the locker room for a new jersey, they just threw him a red shirt. I didn't know that until he hit me. I remember the coach looking down at me and asking, "Where does it hurt, son?"

"My left leg, my right leg, my arms," I started to say. Then I looked up at him and said, "Coach, I hurt all over."

It was only bruises, but I missed three or four games, and when I was ready to rejoin the team, I found out that I wasn't the most welcome man on the field. A sophomore, Willie Matthews, and I had both been injured before the season, and we were ready to come back at the same time. We'd both been listed on the team's insurance policy—a team could only insure thirty-three boys—and we'd already been hurt and treated. So Mr. Rhodes had to keep us on the team unless we resigned voluntarily. Willie didn't want to quit, and neither did I. The coach did his darndest to persuade us.

Mr. Rhodes had a couple of older fellows who weren't on the insurance list. He thought they could help County more than we could. So he called a meeting of the whole team, stood Willie and me up in front, and told everybody what lousy football players we were, how selfish we were, and how we were making two older guys give up the game because we wouldn't quit. He rapped us pretty good. Matthews quit right there. Jones didn't.

I was barely fifteen years old, and I guess I didn't even know when I'd been humiliated. All I wanted to do was play football. After having to convince Mama Myrt to let me play, I wasn't going to allow a little speech by the coach make me turn in my uniform. Of course, I really couldn't give up my uniform that year because I never actually got one, not a complete game uniform, anyway. The last few guys on the bench had to piece together their uniforms. Before the games I used to take shoe polish and draw my number on the front and the back. I only got in for three or four plays all season.

But I was too young to let any of that bother me, and I don't even remember feeling too bad about not making the road trips. They only took me along on one trip all through my freshman year, to Baldwin County, which was about thirty miles away. You could only feed so many kids on a trip like that. I was the only one on the team that didn't play in that game, and I was the only one who didn't eat after that game.

You learned humility before you learned much about football, the way things went at County. Coach Rhodes always said that freshmen were lower than dirt, and then he went out of his way to prove it. He taught you a few things about being a man in addition to being a football player, and he's still doing it.

Mr. Rhodes was a stern man, very demanding, but very popular. At practice he used to walk around with a big paddle in his right hand. And if a player didn't go all out throwing his block or making a tackle, Mr. Rhodes had an effective means of letting him know about it.

When I was in school, there wasn't much excuse for a man doing things wrong or not trying his hardest. I mean, we had just too much talent on the field, no matter what the season was. And it wasn't just Agee and me, not at all. I can think back to some of the guys who never had the chance to try pro ball but were about as talented as we were as high school players. One name in particular stands out in my mind: James Bratley.

Bratley was a year or two older than I was, so it could be that I idolized him a little. He was a better baseball player than me. He could hit a ton and play every position well. But the pro scouts weren't exactly catching every inning of our games. I ran into Bratley again when I played for the Mets' farm team in Buffalo, New York, a few years ago. He works at the Ford Motor Company plant up there, and the job must be a good one, because there aren't too many guys from Plateau who would or could stand those kinds of winters.

My sophomore year, Mr. Rhodes tried me at quarterback, but that didn't last too long. Willie Matthews, the same guy who'd quit the team the year before, got the position. The second-string passer was Bennie Crenshaw, who went on to star at Grambling and then to tryouts with both the Giants and the Jets.

Before the season actually started, I was the regular right halfback. I liked that better than quarterback anyway because it gave me a chance to run and block more, and I didn't mind contact, so long as I was the one making the contact. I didn't care for anybody hitting me very much. In fact, I used to say that the reason I ran so well wasn't because I was good. It was because I was afraid.

But I did love to tackle and block, and of course almost everything we did was fun. It always is when you win. And we won. Each season from my sophomore year on we lost only one or two ball games at County. The big game was traditionally Thanksgiving Day—Mobile Central versus Mobile County, ten thousand fans on hand.

Central had some good football teams over the years. Willie McCovey and the Aaron boys graduated from Central, and how many other high schools in the United States can say they produced men who finished first (McCovey) and third (Hank Aaron) in the National League's Most Valuable Player voting? But during the years I was at County, we were better. We lost, 14–12, in my freshman season, but we won three straight from them after that.

We scored 143 points and gave up only two touchdowns in our first four games my junior year. We had a fine line and backs with real speed—myself, Leon Dozier, and Mitchell Edwards. We hardly had to pass at all, our running game was so effective. It got so the other teams stacked up nine and ten men against the run, and that's when we had real fun: the 49-option. I'd get the ball on a halfback rollout, and Agee, the end, would fake a block at the line of scrimmage and beat his man downfield. I hit him for seven or eight touchdowns with that play.

In my senior year at County we had another fine team, and we did well. I scored twenty-six touchdowns that season.

Of course, as good as the team was at County, so far as the rest of the community was concerned, we were only a good *black*

team, and I was only a good *black* player. We didn't play any
white schools then; we had to travel all over the Southeast for
games, even though there were plenty of white schools sitting
right across town. We weren't allowed to mix on the field.

We used to talk about that when I was in high school. I remember there was a school in Mobile called Vigar High, a white
school that had pretty good teams in those days. We'd speculate
on what we would do against them. I believe we would've done
O.K. Our track team, for instance, had a lot of sprinters who
could run the 100-yard dash in under 10 seconds. We'd read
about a white track meet in the paper with someone winning
the 100 in 10.3. When you saw things like that, you'd say,
"Damn, those white boys wouldn't have a chance with us." But
you didn't think about it to the point where you'd say, "We
should be able to play against those guys." I mean, it just wasn't
going to happen. Not in Mobile, Alabama, in the 1950's.

In fact, we'd played against white boys when we were younger.
But only the kids knew about those games. Some of our guys
worked in the supermarkets in town right alongside some of the
white kids. One group would hear the other talking football or
baseball, and it wouldn't be long before they'd get a game up.
We used to sneak off into the woods to play those games, because if anyone had seen us, they might've called the police to
break it up. As far as the games went, I don't recall that they
were any different from the other games we played back then.
There was no hassle, no name-calling or anything like that. We
got along. I know I never thought about color so far as sports
were concerned. I just wanted to play. I never hated a white
man because he was white. But I did hate some whites for some
of the things they did to us. Sometimes we'd be coming back
from downtown or a neighboring section like Magazine Point
or Toulminville, and some white boys would go by in cars and
yell and throw things at us and try to run us off the road. Sometimes their cars actually hit someone, ran him over. On purpose.
If one of our guys was riding a bicycle, they'd try to force him
off the road and wreck the bike.

That sounds pretty awful when I think about it, even today.
But you know, we were brought up in that kind of atmosphere,

and at the time it was different. I was never a very inquisitive kid to begin with, in school or anywhere else. If someone told me, "Don't go in the front of the store because we don't allow colored people up there," that was all I needed to know. I didn't ask why. I didn't have to. I was black. It was that way, and I knew it. I couldn't change it, and I didn't see anyone else trying to change it. It didn't upset me. And it may sound funny, but in spite of all that, I always felt that Mobile was a fairly liberal town. I know it's hard for people to hear the kind of things that happened to me when I was a kid and then hear me say that Mobile wasn't that bad. But remember, Mobile was on the coast. I had a pretty good idea of what life was like for black people a couple of hundred miles inland.

Mobile is a shipping town, and the business the port brought in made the town more prosperous than the areas up in the Black Belt. Up there a man who sharecropped, for instance, was totally dependent for his living on one white farmer. We were second-class citizens in Plateau, but at least we had the chance to fend for ourselves a little. There was more opportunity for work, and there were more things to enjoy.

A youngster growing up today probably finds it hard to believe that we had no militant thoughts. I think that's a good sign, because it shows how much has happened in this country in just fifteen or twenty years, how far we've come. And there's still a lot more to be done. Maybe a lot quicker.

Perhaps because you get used to a way of life, I loved Plateau. Tommie Lee and I went to Chicago to visit my father several times. They were pleasant trips, but I couldn't wait to get back home. I missed the kids in Plateau and the slower life there. But mostly, I guess, I missed Mama Myrt.

Now when I think back to all she did for us, I'm amazed. As a kid you don't really give much thought to these things. There were times when we'd go to school and somebody would say, "Oh, that's a mighty fine shirt you have on," or "Oh, your slacks are looking good." Now I realize that every outfit Tommie Lee and I had was one that Mama Myrt went without.

You know, I look back and my reaction is, "How in heck did I make it? Could I ever go through that again?" I know I wouldn't want my kids to go through it. But it's a funny thing, our four-year-old daughter, Anja, always seems happier in Plateau than she does in New York.

In fact, the first place Angela and I think about going when we have a couple of free weeks is home to Plateau. And now I can do all the things I want down there. Most of all, I go fishing. Every day.

All of my people were good fishermen, and they have been for generations. When I was small, my great-grandmother took me fishing in the creeks and rivers that feed into Mobile Bay. She would row the boat herself, and she seemed to know just where to find the fish. Those were good days for me and bad days for the fish. If we didn't catch anything, all we had for dinner was greens and beans. But I don't remember that happening very often.

When I went fishing, I'd yell back into the house, "Heat the skillet, I'm going fishing." After Angela and I were married, she spotted me one day in the fish market after I'd been out on the water all day. Do you know what that woman thought? She actually thought I hadn't caught anything and I was trying to buy some fish for supper. I set her straight. "Honey," I told her, "I caught so many fish today that we couldn't possibly eat them all. So I figured I'd come down here and sell the extras."

4

Going, Going, Gone . . .
for $10,000

I always wanted a career in athletics. I didn't care whether it was football or baseball, but I knew I wanted to be a professional. Whenever I had to get up in front of a class and talk about my ambitions, it was always "I want to be a professional ballplayer like Jackie Robinson or Roy Campanella."

I never thought about color when I chose my heroes. As I said, I started switch-hitting as a kid because Mickey Mantle did. Nobody ever asked me, "Why do you like Mantle? He's a white man." I liked him because he was a great ballplayer. I liked Joe DiMaggio for the same reason. But in front of those classes I'd only talk about black athletes, because then a distinction had to be made. For me to get up and say, "I want to be like Stan Musial," would have been as meaningless in those classrooms in Plateau at that time as it would have been for me to say, "I want to be the Mayor of Mobile," or "I want to be President of the United States."

There were one or two black football heroes, but most of the time, when I was a kid, the only real name was Jackie Robinson. He'd been the first. He was the symbol. We even had a song: *"See Jackie Robinson hit that ball/Hit it across the left-field wall."* Of course, you also heard about Campanella. But Jackie was the main man.

I never saw those guys play, but just the same, I knew I

wanted to be like them if I could. I used to ask myself, "Am I going to be good enough to play the way they do?"

And I also wondered, "Am I going to get the chance?"

Sports probably kept me in school. I wasn't a bookworm, and if I have pleasant memories of my earlier days in school, it's probably because of the things I associated with it rather than the school itself. I enjoyed going to grade school because there were always ball games—before class, during lunch recess, and after school.

Once, I played hooky for half a year. Not a day or a week, but a semester, a half-year. And I might still be playing hooky from one thing or another, doing God knows what, if it hadn't been for a wonderful lady named Mrs. Valina McCants, a teacher at County High School.

It was my freshman year, or what should have been my freshman year, at County when I got in with a bad group of guys and started cutting up. I'd start out for school in the morning and wind up somewhere else, anywhere else. Some days they'd find us and try to punish us, but they couldn't really do anything to keep us in school short of locking us in the building.

Then I met Mrs. McCants. She was a history teacher then. Now she's a guidance counselor. Right off, her attitude was different from the others. I'm sure the other teachers had tried to help me, but Mrs. McCants broke through. When she spoke to me, it wasn't just a bunch of words. She was the type of person who made you believe her. She was able to put me in the right frame of mind.

Of course teaching isn't only sitting behind a desk and talking at a kid. And Mrs. McCants appreciates that. Once, after I'd missed a day, the next morning she showed up at the house. Mama Myrt had awakened us and then, after she'd left for work, I'd found my way back to the bed. The next thing I felt was someone shaking me, good and hard, and I looked up and saw Mrs. McCants. She started coming by regularly after that, making sure I got to school. And, although I'm not sure how I felt on some of those mornings, today I love her for it very much.

One of the proudest moments in my life was the day Mrs.

McCants came to New York City, in 1969, to watch me play in
the World Series.

I had some good teachers in high school, but I'm afraid they
didn't have much to work with. I was twelve years old in 1954,
the year of the Supreme Court integration decision, and Mobile
was a little slow to react to that decision. In 1970 the county was
still fighting to keep the schools segregated.

In a different environment I probably could have gotten interested in studying at a much earlier age. As a kid, you see
other kids playing hooky. Maybe they're a year or two older
than you are, and you immediately think that's the thing to do.
You think, "He's getting away with it." So you try. And if you're
caught and punished, that's OK because the school can't erase
the memory of the good time you had.

On school days my grandmother left the house for her job at
County High at six thirty every morning—but only after putting
our breakfast on the table. When you're poor, you want to get
as much food in you as soon as you can. In the mornings we
always had our hominy and our grits with biscuits and mo-
lasses. We always ate plenty. There wasn't meat every day—or
even once a week—but we never went hungry. We always had
our greens and beans. We didn't call it soul food then. It was
all the food we knew. I told people years later that I always
thought fatback was steak until after I'd signed my first pro
contract.

I was kidding, of course, but that wasn't very far from the
truth. Chicken was the big thing for special occasions, with
maybe turkey or meat loaf sometimes. When I was young, we
raised chickens at home, and we even had a few hogs for a while.
But instead of feeding the chickens or slopping the hogs, I liked
to go out in the yard and throw something, try to hit a target.

Everything revolved around sports. I even found my wife because of football in high school. I'd spent very little time with
girls. I was pretty shy. But all the guys thought I had a lot of
girlfriends. I was scoring the touchdowns, so they naturally assumed I was a Casanova. It wasn't that way at all, although I
did get more apples than anyone else on the team.

At County High, it was a tradition for the girls to bring

apples with them to the games. After the game each girl would present an apple to the fellow on the team she liked most. I usually got more apples than I could carry, but most times that was as far as my romantic adventures went. The other guys were after more than apples, I guess. But I could never seem to maintain interest in the few girls that I did date. I'd tire of the same girl very quickly—until I met Angela. It's going on ten years now, and I'm not tired yet.

Angela was fourteen years old and a freshman at County High the year I was a senior, and she brought an apple to one of the games. But she was afraid to come over and give it to me, so she sent a friend over. Her friend gave me the apple and pointed out Angela, a very pretty little girl who looked shy and embarrassed.

Angela lived in Whistler, which was a couple of miles from Plateau. Tommie Agee grew up in Whistler, and a few years before, one of the all-time County High stars, Billy Williams, had grown up there. Billy and Angela are second cousins. I used to enjoy walking over to Angela's house (about a two-mile stroll) because her family had a television set. I used to drop by her house and watch TV all night. Her family didn't know what to make of it. I'd walk in the door, nod, say something softly to Angela, and then sit next to her in the living room and watch the programs. There were whole nights when I didn't say more than hello and good-bye.

But I loosened up after a while. One night, after we'd been dating for a few months, Angela's family had a barbecue. I made quite an entrance. I pulled a big yellow sheet off a clothesline, put it over my head, and hid in the bushes at the edge of her backyard. Someone heard rustling in the bushes and walked over to see what the noise was. I jumped out at him. They didn't see the humor in that at first. But after a while they all thought it was pretty funny, almost as funny as my telling them a few months later that Angela and I wanted to get married.

By then I'd known her for almost a year, an important year for me. In addition to scoring twenty-six touchdowns and batting over .400 at County High, I'd started to think about college. Charles Rhodes, my football coach, and Curtis Horton, my baseball coach, had me interested in college for what it could do for me both as a person and as a ballplayer.

You hear about the pressure put on athletes by big-time white college recruiters. I was never recruited by any of those schools, of course, but I can't believe that they could possibly be any more competitive than the Negro colleges in the south. I started out in June on a football scholarship at one college, was persuaded in August to transfer to another, made the transfer, was re-recruited less than a week later by the original school, then kept spinning around, heading first in one direction and then the other like a target in a shooting gallery.

My college travels started with Alabama Agricultural and Mechanical College, which had always attracted a lot of players from County High.

Alabama A&M played a fair brand of football. The very good players went to bigger schools like Southern University. And the best went to Grambling. That's where Agee had gone, and that's where the coaches at County wanted me to go. They said I'd be seen by all the scouts there, that I'd pick up a good-sized bonus in either football or baseball, that at Grambling I'd be playing in the big time.

I left for Grambling shortly after I graduated from high school. They were going to give me special courses in the summer to get me a head start on my college work. I was never happy there, mostly I think because I'd never been away from home for any length of time. The people at Grambling must have noticed my homesickness right away, because Eddie Robinson, the football coach, kept asking me what was wrong. Rob knew that I told all the guys about Angela, and he made a point of telling me that he didn't mind having married players on his teams. He said, "If you want to, bring her down. We'll get special quarters for you and her." I went back to Plateau for a weekend and sat down with Angela's parents and told them that I wanted to marry their daughter and take her back to Grambling with me. Angela hadn't started her sophomore year in high school yet. Her parents thought I was crazy.

"How can you support our daughter?" her mother asked me. "You can't even support yourself." Somehow, I couldn't convince them that you could play college football for a living. I went back to Grambling disappointed. About that time, the fellows from County who'd gone to Alabama A&M started writing me at Grambling, saying how nice it was with so many guys from Mobile up there. "Why don't you come to A&M?" the letters asked. "If you come here, we'll have a great football team. The coach wants you, but he doesn't think he can get you away from Grambling."

Grambling was *the* school—the Notre Dame of the black colleges (though it's been integrated since then). There are more men from Grambling playing pro football today than from Notre Dame. Tommie Agee played baseball there for only a year or two and got $65,000 from the Cleveland Indians. Grambling was definitely where the money was, and it was also a good academic school. That may have troubled me, too. I knew there were things I wasn't equipped to do. I couldn't be a chemist or a mathematician because I didn't have the groundwork. And in my courses at Grambling that summer, things seemed awfully strange.

Actually, it was a great opportunity I had at Grambling, in sports, in classes, every way. But I was young and in love and homesick, so I didn't have much perspective that summer of 1961. I told my roommate, Joe Reese, that I was leaving for good, and I packed and left. I contacted some of the guys at Alabama A&M and they said they'd come down to Plateau and pick me up.

I went home, saw Angela and my family, and drove up to A&M. I got there, stayed a week, and decided I wanted to go back to Grambling. A lot of people from back home kept telling me that I was too good a football player to stay at A&M when I could play for Grambling and maybe be a star. I thought about it, and I guess the fact that I was just as far away from home in Normal, Alabama, as I had been in Grambling, Louisiana, also sunk in. I called Eddie Robinson and told him I wanted to go back.

Rob told me, "Hold on a second. Stay right where you are and give me the number. I'll call you right back." He hung up, contacted Dr. Jones, Grambling's president (and baseball coach), and called me back. He said, "Get on a train, get on a bus, get on anything you can, and get right back down here."

So I went home again to Plateau, saw Angela and my family, and was about to start out for Grambling when Charles Hope got hold of me. Hope had graduated from County the year before I did, and he was one of the guys who'd convinced me to leave Grambling for A&M. Now, when Louis Crews, A&M's football coach, heard I'd left, he sent Charles Hope out after me. He came down, caught me, and said, "Look, man, we need you up there, and the coach likes you. They're going to buy all your books up there and everything."

That was another thing. Grambling was the rich school. They weren't giving out full scholarships at A&M. But Hope told me I wouldn't have to pay for a thing. Even a couple of deans had decided they would chip in for my books and supplies. So it was back up to Normal.

Charles had taken the train down to catch me, and that's the way we went back. Somehow, the railroad lost all my luggage. They still haven't found it. When I got up to Huntsville, all I had were the clothes on my back and a couple of things I'd packed in a small bag and carried aboard. I was tired, confused, upset; I called back down to Grambling and told Rob I wanted to come back, but I didn't have any clothes. He said, "Come on down, we'll meet you in town and buy you all the clothes you need."

I started out for the bus depot when Coach Crews caught up with me. He told me A&M would make up for the clothes I'd lost. I guess the merry-go-round had to stop somewhere, and they really did want me there, so I told him I'd stay at A&M.

I began classes at Normal and tried catching up to the football team, which had been practicing all the while I was going back and forth between Grambling, Mobile, and Normal. At least, I figured, that's the end of this recruiting thing.

Our first game was only a few days away, in Nashville against Fisk University on a Saturday afternoon. I wasn't familiar enough with our offense to play regularly. All I could do was run back kicks. I ran two kickoffs and a punt back for touchdowns, which wasn't a bad day. And when the final gun sounded and I started for the dressing room, I heard a familiar voice call, "Hey, Beep, Beep." That was my Grambling nickname—sort of a tribute to my running style.

I turned around, and it was Eddie Robinson. Grambling had a game in Nashville against Tennessee A&I that night, and he had come to our game.

"Come on back down," Rob told me, as I stood right there on the field in my Alabama A&M uniform. "You'll have to sit out a year now, but the way you can run that football, I'll get you a lot of money."

Then Rob went into our dressing room and talked to Crews. He said that Grambling had a real good football team and he really wanted me. Crews told Rob thanks, but he wanted me, too, and he had me. That was it.

Ironically, after all that I only got to play a single season of college football. I signed a professional baseball contract the following summer and went back to Alabama A&M, but only as a student, in 1962. And I didn't play too much that first year because it took time to learn the plays. On top of that I hurt my back while blocking. But there was one game, against Miles College of Birmingham, that I'll never forget.

I'd hurt my back the week before, and even though I suited up, the coach never expected me to play in the Miles game. I sat out the first half, and it was a close game. At half time, when we were going over our plays and discussing what would work in the second half, I got up and said, "Coach, if you need me, I'm ready."

In the fourth quarter we were down 14–12, and we weren't moving the ball at all. Everybody in the stands on our side of the field stood and started yelling, "We want Cleon. . . . We want Cleon. . . . We want Cleon." And on the sidelines our players started saying, "Let him go, coach. He wants to play." There were only three minutes or so left in the game, and finally Crews walked over to me and said, "Jonesy, get out there."

When I ran out, we were on our own 33-yard line. The quarterback gave me the ball on the first play. It was like make-believe. I found the hole, made a cut, and just kept running.

I went 65 yards to the Miles 2-yard line. When it was over, I suddenly remembered my back. It hurt. I came out after that one play, but we scored two plays later and won the game.

I enjoyed playing football, but after my freshman season at Alabama A&M, I was fairly certain that if I got the chance, I'd sign a professional baseball contract. For one thing, even though I was convinced that a college education was important, I knew that I'd rather be a professional athlete than an industrial arts teacher (which was what I was studying to be). And while I liked the idea of playing pro football, I still had three varsity seasons before I could even be drafted by a professional team.

Besides, Agee had just signed with the Indians for a $65,000 bonus, and I felt I was in Tommie's class as a baseball player. Angela and I wanted to get married, and if I could get that kind of money, we'd be able to do that and still have enough left over to make things easier for Mama Myrt. By then Tommie Lee had married and moved out, and it was time, if we could, to start saying thank you to our grandmother.

And there's no denying that as serious as I tried to get about school, my heart was still back in Plateau. I remember that I used to sneak off whenever I could and head for home. I wouldn't call or anything. I'd just show up. Angela probably suspected that I was missing classes, but she was so happy to see me that she didn't ask questions. I got home any way I could, usually by talking one of the guys with a car into joining me. It didn't take much talking to drum up a carload of Mobile kids. Those trips were something—one in particular I'll never forget. I know five other guys who'll never forget it, either.

I didn't have a driver's license then. The big thing in my neighborhood was whether you could afford a *bicycle*. But a couple of the older fellows had cars at Alabama A&M, and one weekend six of us piled into one and headed home. Everybody was pretty tired. The other guys could drive, but it was a long ride from Normal to Mobile, 325 miles without any thruways. Finally, there were four guys asleep, and the guy at the wheel said he felt beat. I asked him if he wanted me to drive. He said, "Do you know how?" I said, "Sure." He pulled over to the side of the road and changed places with me.

I'd never driven a car before. Not even down the block. But I hit the accelerator, and we got going. The guy I'd switched places with fell asleep right away, so I was the only one awake in the car. And I was discovering that driving wasn't so hard at all. The farther we went, the better I felt and the faster I drove. And the faster I drove, the better I felt.

Finally, my friend Ike Kidd woke up in the back seat. Ike was sitting next to Charles Hope, and they were the two guys in the car who knew that I'd never driven before. We were going 100 miles an hour and taking the curves pretty strong. I caught some motion in the rear. It was Ike, shaking Charles as hard as he could and yelling, "Hey, look who's driving!" In a few seconds they were both awake, leaning forward, pounding my back and screaming for me to stop the car. I pulled over to the side and tried to look as innocent as I could.

"You can't drive," Charles yelled at me. By now all the guys were awake.

"Sure I can drive." I told them. "What do you call what I've just been doing?"

Charles got out of the car and moved around to the driver's side, and I could tell it was no time to be funny. I started to slide over and said, "I'll sit next to you."

"The hell you will!" Kidd said from the back seat. For the rest of the trip they wouldn't even let me in the front of the car.

Most of my rides home weren't as adventurous as that one, but they all got me there. And the more I saw of home and Angela, the more I wanted to get married and become a baseball player full time. Then, that spring, there was another incident with an automobile, not nearly as funny or as pleasant as my joyride on Route 31. This happened right in Plateau, and I wasn't driving. In fact, the car I was in wasn't even moving.

I had just returned from college, and I was with a fellow named Charlie Caldwell, a friend of mine, when a guy named Jesse drove by. Jesse had borrowed a wheelbarrow from me some time before, and I asked him when he was going to return it. He said, "Get in the car and we'll drive to where I have it and I'll give it back to you." I said OK and got in. We hadn't moved when a car came down the street and hit us head on.

Jesse slammed into the steering section. I went through the windshield.

When Caldwell ran up to the accident, I was trying to get out of the car. He came around to my side, and I told him, "Help Jesse, I'm all right." I didn't feel any pain, though my face felt very wet. I thought I was perspiring a lot.

"Lie down, man," Caldwell told me. "You're hurt."

I insisted that I was OK, but by this time my grandmother had come running out of our house and up the street. She started screaming the moment she saw me. That convinced me something was wrong. I looked down and for the first time realized that I wasn't sweating. I was bleeding. The blood was gushing down my face. I lay down, and someone put towels on my face and got me to the hospital.

There was still no pain, and despite all the blood I'd seen, I didn't think I was hurt that badly. I was being wheeled into an elevator at the hospital, and one of the attendants said, "Doctor, what do you think? Do you think he will be all right?"

The doctor said, "If we can stop the bleeding, we can save him." It didn't sink in for a few seconds. Then it did. Save me. *Save* me? I knew I was hurt. I was frightened.

The doctors at Mobile General Hospital stopped the bleeding and sewed me up. The glass had ripped my face open and I'd lost an awful lot of blood. My life was on the line, and they did a magnificent job. The doctors were white men and I was a black kid, but at the moment of crisis that didn't matter at all. It never does. I found that out on the operating table and on the sandlots before that and all over the country since. There are always some people, on both sides, who try to make color matter. But they're working against human nature. A man is a man.

That night at Mobile General my life was saved when the doctors stopped the bleeding, and my career was saved when they saved my eye. The operation left a permanent scar on the right side of my face, but I can't get too upset about the scar because whenever I become aware of it, I realize how lucky I am to be alive and to be a ballplayer.

At the time, though, I have to admit that the scar bothered

me a lot. And it also showed me what kind of friends I had, because none of them made anything of it. The day after the accident Angela visited me in the hospital. She was only in the tenth grade then, but we knew that someday we would marry.

Angela came to see me with a cousin of hers. She entered the room and stood at the door for a few seconds. We looked at each other. Her cousin whispered to her to walk over to me, and after a few more seconds she did. She kissed me and told me how sorry she was that it had happened and how happy she was that I was all right. I looked a mess, and we both knew that, but more important, we both knew it didn't matter. We loved each other more than ever.

I stayed in the hospital about a week, and then I spent a few more weeks recuperating at home. After a while I began feeling better each day. I started throwing a baseball around, and by the middle of the summer you never would have known I'd been in the accident if not for the scar. I was playing ball again, and I was happy, but I was also more restless than ever. I wanted to sign.

This was just a year or so before the major leagues' free agent draft rule. Today a prospect is selected by one of the teams, and he must sign with that one team or wait until the next selection meeting six months later. But in those days you could sign with any team you wanted to.

Years before that, when there were no rules at all, the teams each spent hundreds of thousands of dollars bidding on the top ballplayers coming up out of high school. But then the majors put in another rule that ended most of that. The rule said that if a rookie wasn't elevated to the major league spring training roster after his first season in pro ball, he could be drafted for only $8,000. That put a squeeze on the market for guys like me.

Since there were only forty men on each roster, everybody below that in each organization could be drafted—$8,000 for first-year players, $12,000 for second-year players, and $25,000 for veterans. Once a team added up the twenty-five men it had the year before, the top prospects from its minor-league teams, and the men it had signed recently, there were only one or two new openings each season. So each team would go sky high for

one or two top prospects—guys it felt couldn't miss making the
majors—and the rest of us would be offered about $10,000 to
sign. If a $10,000-bonus baby was drafted, hardly any money
was lost. But if a team shelled out $50,000 for a kid and then
couldn't find room for him and lost him for $8,000, it was out
a lot of money.

Agee looked like a major-league center fielder at Grambling,
and the Indians signed him. He was one of their can't-miss kids.
But I wasn't that advanced as an outfielder, despite my arm and
my speed. I could hit very well, but you can only guess how well
a young player will hit when he gets his first taste of major-
league pitching. So although a number of teams approached
me—the Giants, the Cardinals, the Cubs, and the Red Sox—
nobody ever talked big money.

The Mets had never spoken to me. And maybe they never
would have if it hadn't been for a friend of mine, Clyde Gray.
Clyde was a few years older than I was. He played semipro with
me. He was a first-baseman and a good power hitter, but he'd
never gotten the chance to play pro ball. One night he and his
wife were talking about it in their living room when my name
came up. Both of them said it would be a shame if I never got
a chance at pro ball.

Clyde turned to his wife and said, "There's no use sitting
here and talking; I'm going to do something about it. I'm going
to write a couple of people about that boy." This was before my
accident, in the spring, and the teams were at training camps.
Clyde tried to figure out which teams needed hitters, and he
finally wrote to the Kansas City Athletics and the Mets.

He sent one letter to Hank Bauer, who was then managing
at Kansas City, and one to Casey Stengel, who had just become
the manager of the Mets. Bauer never answered his letter.
Neither did Casey. He did better than write back. A few weeks
after Clyde wrote, he got a call from Julian Morgan, a Met scout.

Morgan saw me play in one of our semipro games that summer—sort of. The day he came it rained, and we only got two
innings in. He saw me throw and swing a bat in practice. But
that was about all. Morgan told me he'd like to see more of me.
He also wanted one of the other scouts to look me over. He said

that the team's nearest farm club was in Salisbury, North Carolina, and that was where he wanted me to work out. Morgan
asked me if I could meet him in Atlanta the following week
so we could drive from there to Salisbury. Clyde told me he'd
drive me the 350 miles to Atlanta, and Morgan said he'd take
the two of us to North Carolina, about 200 miles from there.
We made an appointment.

We were supposed to meet him at a railroad depot outside
Atlanta, and I guess when the day came, I was pretty excited.
Clyde and I left extra early and made good time. We got there
two hours before we were supposed to. And Morgan showed up
an hour late.

We went straight to Salisbury and stayed three days. I was
an amateur, so I couldn't play in the games, but I took batting
and fielding practice, and I felt I did well. I could hardly have
done poorly compared to some of the players they had there.
If you remember what those early Met teams looked like, you
can imagine what their lowest farm teams had in the way of
talent. I felt pretty cocky after my workouts, figuring I had to
be worth a lot of money. I figured wrong.

Morgan offered me $850 a month and a $10,000 bonus. I
didn't have to go to North Carolina for that kind of offer. I told
him to forget it and said I was going back to Plateau. Morgan
told me to hold my horses. He'd try to raise the offer. On the
way back to Atlanta he stopped and made a few phone calls.
But each time, he returned to the car with the same story, that
all he could give me was $850 a month plus the $10,000. I said
no, thank you, I was going home.

Morgan dropped us off at the depot, and we drove back to
Plateau a little more leisurely than we had driven on the way
to Atlanta. When I got home, Julian Morgan was waiting for
me. He told me that I could make it big and that he wanted to
sign me. He told me that the only way I could get more money
was to go to New York and work out in front of the club officials. He said he'd get plane tickets for me and my grandmother.

I told him we'd go to New York, but I was bluffing. I knew
nobody on this earth would ever get Mama Myrt inside an air-
plane. Morgan kept talking and talking and talking. He made

another phone call to New York, and then he talked some more. It was all part of the game the major-league teams play. He knew I wanted to sign and that sooner or later he would wear me down. There ought to be a rule that says a kid can't talk to a team without a lawyer in the room. Finally, I agreed to sign. I settled for $850 a month plus $10,000, exactly the original offer.

5

Big Tipper from Mobile

By the time I signed with the Mets in the summer of 1962, it was too late for me to play that season in the minor leagues, so I made plans to enroll at Alabama A&M for the fall semester and gain a few more credits toward an industrial arts degree. I was back up at Normal when I got a call from Joe MacDonald, the Mets' farm director. He told me the club wanted to get its first long look at me in the Florida Instructional League.

The Instructional League is an informal month-long session in Florida where a team can get a line on some of its younger players and try out a veteran or two at different positions. It's a good idea, because all the coaches can pay attention to youngsters they might not have time for once the regular spring training begins.

Because the Mets were barely a year old, most of the guys on our Instructional team were kids like myself. The big club had a 40–120 record in its first season, and the idea was to find some kids who could play. It was my first try at organized ball.

Right from the start, I could see a difference between even the Instructional League and the best semipro games I'd been in. When I first got to St. Pete, I wasn't throwing the ball as hard or straight as some of the other outfielders. That upset me because I'd always thought I had a good arm. One day Solly Hemus, a Met coach, asked me if I was holding the ball with the seams or across the seams.

"The seams?" I asked Solly. "I never really noticed."

Solly explained that if I threw the ball with my fingertips across the seams, I'd get more power and control.

Little Leaguers learn that when they're eight years old. But it had never occurred to me back in Plateau that the seams were for anything but holding the cover on the ball. By the end of the Instructional League season I was throwing hard and straight, and Jim Hickman and I were rated the two best outfield arms in camp.

I'd played with and against some good pitchers and hitters and fielders before, but there were enough triple-A and major-league players down in Florida that first time for me to appreciate that in pro ball they would all be good. I noticed it most with the pitchers. Almost every one of them threw a slider, which you hardly ever saw on the sandlots.

I didn't really know what a slider was until I went to Florida that winter. It's a cross between a fast ball and a hard curve, a pitch that sets you thinking "fast ball," then at the last moment fades down and away like a curve. A pitcher who consistently throws sliders can give up a lot of home runs, because sliders that are duds come in straight and fast, without the extra speed and action of a fast ball. But, I learned later on, most major-league pitchers don't throw duds very often.

I met Hickman as well as Ed Kranepool and Ron Hunt, two kids the Mets were very high on, down there that fall. But the guy I remember most was an outfielder from California, Paul Blair. I took to Paul right off. I guess opposites attract. I hardly said a word in those days, and Blair never stopped talking. He talked and laughed and talked and laughed some more. Blair hadn't exactly torn the league apart in his first minor-league season, but that didn't stop him from telling anyone who'd listen (and anyone who wouldn't) how great he was going to be. I spoke up when I had something to say, but everything was still strange to me, and I was basically shy. I never liked loudmouths, but when Blair talked, he came off well. It was like a comedy act. This was a guy who loved to brag. That was his game. It wasn't mine.

I was comfortable around Paul, maybe because we could

carry on a conversation for hours and I'd never have to worry about what to say. I'd never get the chance to open my mouth. We roomed together in St. Petersburg, where the Mets' camp was, and after the Instructional League season was over, we told each other that we hoped we could be on the same team the following season. But a few days later he was drafted from the Mets by the Baltimore Orioles. The Mets had protected me and allowed Paul to be claimed. I know some people have wondered if they made the right decision. I think they made a mistake. They should have protected us both: Blair hit .286 in 1969 with 26 homers.

After my first taste of pro ball I went home to visit my family and see Angela, then back down to Dunedin, Florida, where the Met farm teams had spring training. I was assigned to Buffalo of the International League, the highest minor-league team in the organizations. But I realized that I might be dropped lower before the start of the season because I'd never played any pro ball.

When you're at that stage, the biggest thing you fight is yourself, you're so full of uncertainties about ability and what you're getting into. I didn't know whether I belonged or not. I couldn't walk into spring training that first year and say, "I'm going to make a triple-A ball club." I just had no way of knowing how good I was by professional standards.

The Buffalo manager was Kerby Farrell, who'd been a big-league manager at Cleveland a few seasons before. Kerby liked me right off. He knew that the Mets had me figured to start the season in the low minors, but I attracted his attention immediately.

One afternoon the Mets sent a B team over to Dunedin to play an exhibition game against Buffalo. I was in left field for the Bisons, and one of the Mets hit a high drive, away from me. I took off after it, but it didn't look like there was a chance. Then at the last moment I reached out, dove, and came up with the ball. For a while that spring it was all like that. I caught everything hit near me and batted about .400 in our exhibition games.

Farrell told me he'd try to keep me on the Buffalo roster. I guess the International League is so full of major-league retreads and just-misses that the idea of going with a kid whose entire career was ahead of him appealed to Kerby. At first, the club officials were against Kerby's idea of keeping me. But finally he convinced them to play me at Buffalo. Then an old ailment began bothering me, and the chance for a shot at the International League disappeared.

I'd had a hemorrhoidectomy when I was a kid. Some doctors say hemorrhoids are psychosomatic. Maybe so. I could have been nervous that first spring at Dunedin. At any rate, not too long before we were supposed to head North, the hemorrhoids came back. The team doctor examined me, and then the Mets sent me to New York. They said it was just for a checkup.

I'd never seen New York before. I landed at John F. Kennedy International Airport at dinnertime and hailed a cab. The Mets had told me to go to the Hotel Manhattan, where they'd reserved a room for me. At the Manhattan the cab driver took my luggage out and then told me the fare was $6.25. I carefully counted out the exact amount.

"In New York," the cabby told me, "it's customary to tip taxi drivers."

I reached back into my pocket and pulled out a quarter and handed it to him. I figured that was a pretty good tip. He looked at me, looked at the quarter, muttered, "I've got to make a living, too, buddy," and drove away.

I checked into the hotel, had a sandwich in the coffee shop, and then went up to sleep. It was only seven o'clock, but I didn't know anyone in New York, and I was tired. At nine the phone rang. It was Dr. Peter LaMotte, the Mets' team physician. He told me to go to Roosevelt Hospital immediately. They had a bed for me, and I slept at the hospital that night. I remember thinking that it was an awful lot of trouble to go through for a checkup.

The next morning they told me they were going to operate on me at noon. I was a man of few words in those days, too, and I said, "No, you're not."

I told the doctors and some club officials that if I had an

operation, I didn't want to have it in New York, where I know nobody. If I had to be laid up for four or five weeks, I wanted to be in Mobile. I was twenty years old and out of the South for the first time in my life, and they wanted to stick me away in a hospital room for a month or more by myself with nobody I knew within 800 miles. It didn't seem logical to me. But I was to learn through the years that a baseball team's logic is whatever suits the management.

The Mets told me that if I was going to have an operation at all, it would be right then and there in New York, and furthermore, if I didn't agree, they weren't going to send me to Buffalo. The club said I'd have to report to a team in an A league, the lowest classification. They mentioned Auburn. I said, "Fine. If that's the way you feel about it, send me to Auburn." I didn't know where Auburn was, but I knew it had to be better than a hospital room in New York City.

Auburn turned out to be a little town in upstate New York, near Syracuse. The baseball field had rickety wooden stands, and it was still cold in May, and sometimes there wasn't enough hot water in the shower. But at last I was playing baseball for a living. After about three weeks I was hitting .360.

Then the hemorrhoids came back worse than ever. I went to the manager, Dick Cole, and I told him I had to have an operation, that everything I did hurt and I couldn't take it any longer.

For a few days I hadn't been able to run very well, and the day I went to the manager I'd barely been able to get out of bed in the morning. Cole asked me to wait a couple of days because the late Johnny Murphy, then an assistant general manager for the Mets, was due in the Auburn area. That was all I had to hear. Murphy was one of the club officials who'd insisted I stay in New York for the operation. I went to the airport and flew home.

I arrived in Mobile on a Thursday evening, and by Friday I'd been operated on. It was the first of a series of events that was to give me a bad reputation with some people in the Mets' front office, but looking back now, I'm glad I did it. The operation and recuperation were bad enough in Mobile. They would have been unbearable in New York.

The teams think of their players the way the plantation owners thought of their slaves, as property—no more, no less. Sentiment and concern for the individual aren't considered in those carpeted offices where the directors meet. I'll always try to buck that where I can. Of course when you've hit .340, there are suddenly little considerations they have for you.

In the middle of the 1969 season, for example, the Mets gave me a bonus. They called me in and handed me more money than my contract called for. And they wanted to know, "Is there anything else we can do for you, anything you need?" I told them that the way I was going, I didn't want to change a thing. Not a thing.

But in 1963 when I went back to Mobile instead of letting them railroad me into a miserable couple of months in New York, I was only twenty. I was working on instinct alone, and I'm a little proud today that I wouldn't be pushed around. Let them think what they want about me in the front office, so long as they think that I'm a man.

At the time, the Mets let people think that I'd gone AWOL, simply run off without telling anyone where I was going or why. But that wasn't true. I'd told the manager exactly what I was doing, and the club knew where to reach me. The proof is that they did contact me in Plateau. A month after that they called again and told me to report to Raleigh, North Carolina, in the Class A Carolina League, the same league Salisbury had been in the year before. I told them I was under doctor's orders not to play for another two weeks, but they said to go to Raleigh right away even if I couldn't play. They just wanted me there. So I went to Raleigh.

I'd been there, just sitting around, for two days when the Raleigh manager, Clyde McCullough, the former Chicago Cub catcher, told me he needed me in the lineup. They had a doubleheader, and Clyde was a little short on players. I hadn't picked up a bat or thrown a ball in seven weeks. "I don't want you to run full speed or do anything to hurt yourself," Clyde told me. "I just want you to play yourself into shape." Three innings into the first game of the doubleheader, Clyde flashed me a steal sign. I wound up with six hits and three stolen bases in the doubleheader.

I stayed with Raleigh the rest of the season and hit .305 in 49 games. It was a respectable start, and I wasn't unhappy. The highlight of the summer was a visit from Angela. She had come up from Whistler with her mother and stayed for a few days. I was happy about their trip, but before I let them visit, I made certain they could sit near the dugout where the other players' wives and friends sat.

I'm no revolutionary, but I've always stood up for my rights as they affected me. The ball park in Raleigh had a colored section, far down the right-field line. Now I was a ballplayer, and my girl was going to sit where all the other players' friends and relatives sat. I went to the general manager, a good baseball man named Herb Brett, a local man. I didn't tell him to integrate his park. I figured the Negroes in Raleigh must have felt the way I had in Plateau. They just sat there because they were supposed to.

Mr. Brett arranged for Angela to sit with the players' wives, and I told her and her mother to come up. It was great having them around. So in a way, I guess we integrated the park down there. That was seven years ago. Now there isn't a segregated park in the country.

September is an important month to a young minor-leaguer. That's the month the major-league rosters go from twenty-five to forty and the teams bring up fifteen men to play the final few games of the year. I was one of the players the Mets called up. Naturally, I was excited about putting on a major-league uniform. But I was also afraid. You dream about the big league for so long, and then when you're close, you have to stop and wonder if it will really happen. Any kid who says he's sure he has the ability to play in the majors is either lying or silly. A man just doesn't know until he's there.

I reported to the Polo Grounds, where the Mets played for the two years before Shea Stadium opened. The first man I met was Sol Ross, the security guard. He took me in to see the equipment man, who outfitted me with uniforms and assigned me to a locker. Then I left and went back downtown to my hotel room.

The next morning I was back at the Polo Grounds for my first game as a Met. Frank Thomas was the first Met I saw. He was lying on the trainer's table. Frank had been a power hitter with the Pirates and a couple of other National League teams, and he was finishing up his career with the Mets. He had enough power left to hit thirty-four homers for the Mets in their first season, 1962, and it's still a team record. But this was September of his second year in New York, and Frank was near the end; he retired in 1964.

In July, 1969, we were at Forbes Field in Pittsburgh, where Frank Thomas now lives with his family. He walked into our clubhouse, and there I was lying on the trainer's table, looking up at him. The same thought crossed our minds. Frank just shook his head and said, "The years sure go by."

I played in six games in September, 1963, and got two singles in fifteen times up. It wouldn't have been very memorable at all if Casey Stengel hadn't been around. I'd never met Casey. He was something else. Casey was a hero in New York, except with a few commentators. They said he was just a clown who looked and talked funny, that he had no real contact with the young players. But Casey was both helpful and friendly to me, and to this day I've never met a man who knows as much about baseball.

It struck me at the team meeting we had before my first game at the Polo Grounds. In the minors we hadn't had any team meetings. We just discussed things among ourselves on the long bus rides from town to town. But the Mets had a meeting before the first game of each series. Casey would talk about how we should pitch to one guy or how we shouldn't pitch to another guy. He seemed to know something about every man on the other team, no matter how obscure he was.

By September every team we played had guys like me who'd just come up at the end of the season. They'd been playing in the boondocks, but Casey still knew something about them. Somebody would call a guy's name out—"Sonny Jackson"—and

Casey would say, "Oh, he's a fella who can run." "Alley"—"He's the guy with the great arm." And sure enough, if Casey told us the new shortstop had a great arm, the kid would go into the hole, pick up a grounder, and show us a great arm. This is what immediately impressed me about Casey Stengel.

In the games I did play, I was afraid. This was the Polo Grounds, this was where Willie Mays had played. I had to look at myself and say, "Hell, what am I doing here?" I tried to relax, but I was tight.

I admired Mays—and Mantle and Hank Aaron, too—but I never copied anyone else's style. I've always been natural. Before this, I'd played baseball without really thinking about what I was doing. I didn't realize at the time, at least not in so many words, that my natural abilities would only carry me so far. They'd only give me the chance. But I was going to have to learn to practice in order to cash in.

I knew after my first taste in 1963 that I wasn't ready for the big leagues. I knew I was going to report to the Mets' major-league training camp at the start of the 1964 season, but I didn't have any illusions. I expected to go to Buffalo. It would be a step up from Raleigh, and that was what I wanted.

So when I was shipped to Buffalo to start the 1964 season, I was happy. I played well, and the season passed quickly. I went to bat 500 times and hit .278 against triple-A pitching, with 16 homers and 70 runs batted in. It wasn't a sensational year, but I'd just turned twenty-two, and I felt it was a solid season on the way up. In my mind, 1965 was the year I'd get my first good shot at the major leagues.

But I didn't have a very good spring, and when the season started, I was on the Met bench. A few weeks later I was shipped to Buffalo, and it wasn't very easy to take. Angela and I had been married the year before, and I'd sent for her when we got to New York, ready to start my major-league life. Then the day she arrived I was told they were sending me out. It didn't make sense to me. The Mets weren't going anywhere with fading, over-the-hill players. They were building for the future. If they were so committed to youth, they could play me every day in the majors. They didn't see it that way. Casey also was trying to win games, and playing only once in a while, I was only hitting a hundred and something. I was gone.

Until then, every time Angela joined me, starting with the game at Raleigh two years before, I'd had a big game. I hit a homer that first Raleigh game. Then in 1964, the day she came to her first spring-training game, I hit one out. And when she got to Buffalo that year, I homered in my first time at bat. So here she was in New York for the first time, and I had to meet her at the airport and get on another plane with her.

Angela didn't seem to mind, and I tried not to be bitter. I knew the only way to get back was to hit at Buffalo. I figured that if I had an outstanding year on top of the solid one I'd just had in the International League, then they *had* to give me a good shot with the Mets. After six weeks I was hitting .360 with 10 homers. But Sheriff Robinson, the manager at Buffalo, wasn't satisfied. Too many of my hits, he said, even the homers, were going to right and center fields. "When you get up to those big parks in the majors," Sheriff told me, "those shots are going to be long outs. You've got to start pulling the ball more."

Sheriff changed my batting stance and tried to get me out in front of the ball more so I'd hit to left field. More home runs, he said. For the next month and a half I hit exactly one home run. I didn't hit many singles, doubles, or triples, either. I was as down on myself as I've ever been. Three months before, I'd thought I was a major-leaguer. Now I wasn't hitting in the International League. I couldn't understand it. But there was one man in the Met organization who understood what was happening to me, and fortunately, he got a chance to do something about it. The man was Kerby Farrell, the same Kerby Farrell who'd wanted to take me to Buffalo with him two years before.

By the time I got to Buffalo, Kerby had been reassigned. But in the middle of the 1965 season Casey Stengel fell and broke his hip. Wes Westrum became the manager, and Sheriff Robinson became one of his coaches. Farrell replaced Robinson as Buffalo manager.

Kerby called me into his office the day he arrived. He said, "I want things to be just like they were in sixty-three when I first saw you. You're just not hitting the same way you were then. Go back to your old way of hitting. And I want you to start relaxing and let things come easily. Start running the bases the way you can."

It's tough to run the bases, I wanted to tell Kerby, if you can't reach them. But I just thanked him and told him I'd try. Slowly it started coming back. I wasn't trying to pull the ball anymore. I was just trying to make contact. When Robinson left, my average was below .240. I built it up to .269 under Farrell. It was .269 after a .278 in the same league, but sometimes statistics don't tell you everything. I'd overcome something and learned a lot about myself. You have to be what you are, go with your strength. So I wasn't the new Babe Ruth. So what? If I swung naturally and concentrated, I could hit. And good hitters get to play in the majors.

In September I was called up again by the Mets, but I wasn't thinking entirely about baseball. I'd sent Angela back to Plateau a few weeks before. She was expecting our first child at any time. In my hotel room I woke up suddenly at three o'clock on the morning of September 17. I thought I heard Angela's voice, and I jumped out of bed. At that moment, in a hospital in Mobile, Anja Jones was born. Angela had given her mother my phone number in the hotel, but her mother couldn't read the writing and never called me. In the morning I phoned the hospital and found out that I was a father. I asked Angela what she wanted to name our son. She told me that my son was a daughter. We named her Anja because Angela had heard the name watching a beauty contest on television and liked it.

I went back to Mobile two weeks later to see my wife and daughter, then took off for Puerto Rico to play in the Winter League down there. The money wasn't bad, and the Mets thought the extra work would help me. I played for Caguas, which had a number of major-leaguers, including an outfielder from the Mets named Joe Christopher. Joe was one of the few Mets I'd gotten to know in my brief stays with the team. He helped me a lot in Puerto Rico.

I was only hitting .250 when Joe offered me some advice. He said he'd watched me at the plate and that I was swinging too early. I wasn't waiting on the ball. Maybe it was something I

United Press International

" 'Come on down, baby,' I kept saying. 'Come on down.' "

Cleon Jones about to catch the final out of the 1969 World Series.

School Days

1947-48

"I was the type of kid who didn't believe what someone would tell me."

Cleon at six.

"I ran two kickoffs and a punt back for touchdowns, which wasn't a bad day."

Cleon as a freshman halfback at Alabama A&M.

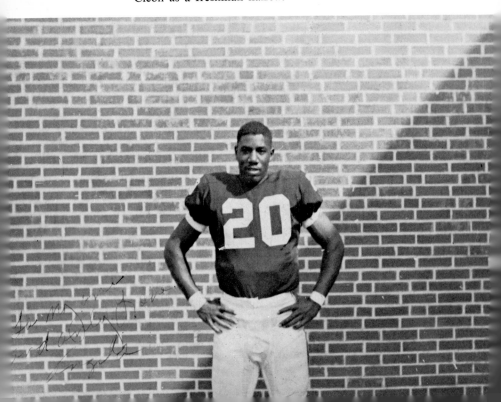

"When you're at that stage, the biggest thing you fight is yourself . . ."
Cleon in his first Met uniform.

"*As soon as I went after a bad pitch, I'd hear from Gil or Eddie Yost or Rube or Yogi.*"

Met coach Yogi Berra, with Roger Maris and Cleon, 1968.

"*The only choice a runner has is to hit him hard and hope the catcher drops the ball.*"

Cleon jars ball from catcher Tom Haller's glove to score.

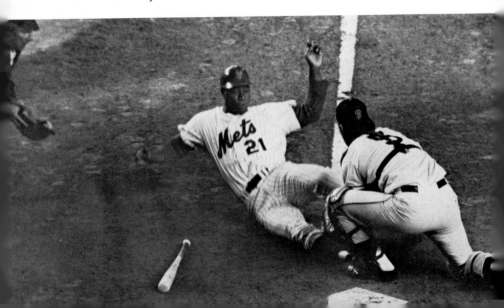

"Sometimes the best trades are the ones you don't make."
Tommie Agee, Cleon, and Al Jackson with Orlando Cepeda, the almost-Met.

"You know, I look back and my reaction is, 'How in heck did we make it?'"
Cleon with fellow Mobile stars Hank Aaron of the Braves (left) and Billy
Williams of the Cubs.

"Our fans were tremendous all season. You wanted to win for yourself, of course, but they made you want to win for them, too."

Young Met partisans leap for joy after a diving, bare-handed catch by Cleon in the left-field corner.

"*A guy like Eddie Kranepool, who speaks his mind, is a pretty good fellow to have around.*"

"I could have hit that last one better with the bat in my back pocket," Cleon tells Met first baseman Ed Kranepool.

"*A ballplayer has to back up his thinking with action.... Without good execution, all the thinking doesn't mean very much.*"

Cleon displays the full force of his swing.

United Press International

"A man can get home run fever easier than he can pick up the Asian flu."
A grand slam, Cleon's first, against the Braves: Boswell, Charles, and Agee
await the soul shake.

hadn't totally lost from the experiment at Buffalo. Bad habits have a way of staying with you at the plate. They become a part of your swing, and they're tough to shake.

Joe told me not to commit myself too early, to stand back and wait until the ball came into what he called "plate focus" before I started my swing. I tried to follow Christopher's advice, and it helped almost immediately. I started taking a more controlled swing, and I began to meet the ball more solidly. I'd taken another step back toward my strength, my natural ability as a hitter. And I knew *why* I was doing *what* I was doing.

Baseball fans know that most power hitters strike out more than the other hitters and also hit more hard grounders and high pop flies than anyone else. In order to get full power they start their swing earlier, committing themselves to thinking the pitch will be in a certain place at a certain instant. If the ball's there, they can hit it out. If it isn't, which is more likely, they'll miss or strike the ball off center. They're still swinging hard, so if they hit over the ball, it's a very hard bouncer. Under the ball, and they hit it a mile high, straight up.

The great power hitters, like Willie McCovey and Harmon Killebrew, are so good that they can be free swingers and still pick up their share of singles. But most hitters have to do it the other way around; we shoot for singles and doubles and pick up our share of homers as they come. There are a few hitters, but only a few, who can go both ways. They have the wrists and reflexes to hit for average and the power to hit the ball out regularly. Ernie Banks, Willie Mays, and Mickey Mantle all did it in their prime, and Hank Aaron is still doing it.

But I'd never shown that kind of power, and in the 1965 season at Buffalo and the winter in Puerto Rico, I realized what I'd have to do to make it in the major leagues. After the winter season finished at Caguas, I went home and took a few weeks off, trying to get ready mentally. I stood in front of a mirror and concentrated on laying back, waiting, then swinging through the imaginary pitch. I talked hitting with Hank Aaron and Billy Williams, two of the best. I figured I was ready, and I only hoped that when I reported to the Mets, I would get a fair chance.

I found out shortly after arriving at St. Pete that I wasn't getting a shot. I was getting a half-shot. Westrum, who hardly knew what I looked like, had already announced to the press that he planned to platoon Johnny Lewis and me in right field. The thought didn't exactly thrill me.

The idea of platooning is that right-handed hitters can see left-handed pitchers better, and left-handed hitters can see right-handed pitchers better. So you load up your lineup with righty hitters against a lefty pitcher and vice versa. If you're fighting for a pennant, looking for every edge, it's not a bad idea. But the Mets were a young team, at least several years away from being a contender, and they were hurting the development of some of their best prospects. You take a Cleon Jones and put him in only against lefties, and pretty soon righties aren't going to be hard for him to hit, they're going to be impossible. I wanted to learn the game, to play under all conditions.

Johnny Lewis and I had known each other for a number of years. He was playing high school ball across the bay in Pensacola when I was at County High, and we played each other a few times. I liked Johnny, and Angela and his wife were close friends that spring. But I just didn't want to platoon. Both of us had good spring-training averages, and Westrum kept shuttling us in and out until shortly after the regular season started. I don't know if I'd shown Wes something or if he'd gotten a phone call from the front office, but after a couple of weeks I became the starting right fielder against all pitchers.

The reason I suspect Westrum was told to play me is because Wes never seemed to think much of my ability. But it was tough to know what Westrum thought of anyone. He hardly ever said anything. You'd have to read the papers to find out what he felt about yesterday's game. He had a habit of just shrugging his shoulders and trying to make you guess what he was thinking. It wasn't the way a man who had to guide young players should act. There was no control. Wes put players in and took them out, just like a manager. But if everything didn't fall into place for us, he blamed everyone except himself.

As a team, we were in the twilight zone. We wanted to forget that old image of the Mets as losers, but nobody would let us. We finished ninth that season—twenty-eight and a half games behind the first-place Dodgers.

It was considered a big accomplishment. We were the first Met team to finish higher than tenth. My high school baseball team had lost one game in three seasons. I wasn't used to losing, and I certainly wasn't ready to accept defeat as easily as it seemed to be taken in the Met clubhouse. Guys would walk in three hours before the game and say, "Oh, well, I wonder how we'll lose today."

I contributed my share of mistakes, as a rookie in 1966, to those losses, but young players are supposed to make some mistakes. The problem with the Mets was that mistakes were expected of everyone. On a winning team you learn from your mistakes. On the Mets we never learned from anything.

I was satisfied with my own season. I finished with a .278 batting average, 57 runs batted in and 74 runs scored. I also stole 16 bases.

After the season, I was picked for the major-league all-rookie team. I figured I was on the way. Maybe I should have known better. Two years before, after that good first year at Buffalo, I'd also assumed too much. Baseball's like a lot of other things. You don't play yesterday's game tomorrow.

I'd never had a bad spring training, and in 1967 I was loose and happy. When the season started, I was playing regularly against right- and left-handed pitchers. But then I went zero for thirteen before I got my first hit. Then I went on another hitless streak. That was enough for Westrum. I was strictly platooned after that.

By the end of May we were dead last and going nowhere. We had a great young pitcher in Tom Seaver and an All-Star second baseman in Ron Hunt and some good young prospects like Bud Harrelson, Ron Swoboda, Ed Kranepool, and myself. We should have been on our way, but instead we were as bad as ever. It was as if we were raising a whole new group of players to follow in the footsteps of the original Mets, the good losers.

The reason, I think, was Westrum. The way he handled me was typical. After my bad start I didn't get coaching. I didn't get reassurance. All I got was a pretty constant seat on the bench. Wes would start me against a left-hander, and if a right-hander came in to relieve in the third inning, I was out of the game. It didn't matter if it was or wasn't a crucial moment; it didn't matter if he had a strong or a weak pinch hitter available. He'd put up any left-handed hitter who happened to be sitting around. If you have the pride of a ballplayer, you can never get used to something like that. Never.

I'll remember one game in Los Angeles that season for the rest of my life. We were down by one run late in the game, and Ron Perranoski had come in to relieve for the Dodgers. Perranoski was a left-hander, so Wes let me hit, and I got a single. Eddie Bressoud came up behind me. Westrum flashed me the hit-and-run sign. Bressoud, the batter, swung and missed. I didn't get a good jump, and I had absolutely no chance of making it to second safely. I tried to dive back into first, the throw beat me, and we eventually lost by one run.

The next morning one of the guys on the team tossed me a copy of the Los Angeles *Times* sports section. I read the story. Then I read it again. I couldn't believe it. Westrum had said it was my fault we'd lost, that I'd missed the sign. He said I'd been missing signs all season and that I'd lost a lot of games for us. He left the general impression that I was an idiot.

I knew I hadn't missed the sign. I also knew that Wes hadn't said a word to me after the game. He never talked to anyone. He was uptight. The team was losing, and he knew he was losing his job. He tried to convince the fans and the writers and the team management that we were just lousy players.

Wes seemed to take it as a personal insult if I played a bad game. He'd badmouth me to the press or smirk when one of the reporters mentioned me by name and point to his head, as if to say that I didn't have it upstairs. He wanted everyone to think that I was stupid, just a dumb colored boy from Alabama who couldn't remember the signs or make decisions.

I wasn't the only one who had a tough time with Wes. Jerry Grote, the catcher, hit .195 and spent half of each game looking over his shoulder to see whether the manager thought he'd called for the right pitch. He had us all jittery and second-guessing ourselves. Jerry might have had it even worse than I did, because Westrum had been a catcher for the Giants, and he seemed to feel nobody in baseball except him knew anything about handling pitchers. Thank goodness he hadn't been an outfielder.

When Wes tried to handle men, he usually didn't do much of a job. Once, on the road, he spotted Swoboda having a drink after curfew. A ballplayer will have a few drinks on occasion. In fact, a little bit of alcohol isn't all bad if it relaxes you and helps put back some of the weight you're losing from the day-to-day grind of a long season.

Wes raced back to the hotel, walked into the lobby, and picked up the house phone to call Swoboda's room. Ed Kranepool, Ron's roommate at the time, answered. "Let me speak to Mr. Swoboda," Wes said. Eddie told him, "He's not here, Skip. I'll tell him you're looking for him." Wes knew Ron was breaking curfew and wasn't there. He'd just run back to the hotel to make the point that he knew Ron wasn't in the room. If Wes had really wanted to talk to Swoboda, all he had to do was walk up to him in the club.

Wes went up to his own room, waited a half hour, and called back. Again Eddie answered. Again Wes asked for "Mr. Swoboda." He was always calling you mister and making it sound snide, as if there were something wrong with your last name. Again Eddie told him, "Sorry, Skip, but Ron isn't back yet. I'll tell him you want to talk to him." Wes waited another thirty minutes and repeated the exact same conversation. He did it again and again.

Finally, when Swoboda got in and Kranepool told him what had happened, he called Wes. "Skip," he said, "I got a message you were looking for me." Westrum sounded half out of his mind. He started yelling at Ron at the top of his lungs. "You're ruining me! You're ruining me!"

Maybe Ron was a little late. But that's what they make managers' offices for. Instead, there was just a lot of shouting over the phone late at night and no words at all the next day. There was also no Swoboda in the Met lineup that day or the next or the next. Wes benched the man for a couple of weeks, and after the shouting match he never said a word to him about it.

It wouldn't have been so bad if we didn't need all the help we could get. We were young, and the guidance wasn't there. I didn't get my average over .200 until August. I'd play one day, sit for two, and play again. One time Wes played me two days in a row, and I told one of the writers that I was planning to send Wes a telegram thanking him. I hoped it would get back. There were times that summer when I felt like running into his office, jumping on his desk, and shouting at him. But I couldn't even whisper anything to Wes Westrum.

There were a couple of men in the clubhouse, veterans, who saw what was happening and tried to keep my spirits up. One was Ken Boyer, the All-Star third baseman we'd picked up from the Cardinals after he started to slow up. The other was Tommy Davis, the former Dodger batting champion. They just told me to keep cool and do my job and not to worry about the man in the office.

"Just don't let Westrum get you down," Boyer told me. "Try to keep your nose clean and you'll pull through. I know you should be playing every day, and so do the other players and the coaches." Ken was trying to tell me what a lot of people knew—that Cleon Jones would be a New York Met long after Wes Westrum was gone, unless I got so mad at him and down on myself that I started to do silly things. If that happened, it would only appear as if Wes had been right all along.

In the end, I just hung in there and tried. Once our general manager, Bing Devine, called me into the office and, in front of Wes, asked me if there was something wrong. I just kept my mouth shut and told him that I was doing my best. He gave me a little pep talk and said I'd play more in the last couple of months of the season. I did. In August I had a thirteen-game hitting streak, and my average kept rising through September. I finished at .246, and I had 101 hits.

In the last week of the season, after a lot of rumors, Westrum resigned. I can't say I was sorry. I remember saying good-bye to Ken Boyer when the season finally ended and thanking him as sincerely as I've ever thanked anybody. I'll never forget how much Boyer's words meant when things were at their worst, and I've tried to repay him the only way I can—by walking over to a young player who's having troubles and making sure he doesn't get down on himself.

6

Confidence Game

After the terrible experience in 1967 I felt I had to get myself together. I decided to go back to Puerto Rico and play winter baseball. Now that I was a major-leaguer, the money was better. I'd received $1,300 a month the first time. Now it was $1,900 a month. And I felt the experience would give me a chance to stay loose, to remember how much fun baseball could be. I went back to Caguas, where I'd made some good friends two years before, and all of a sudden I ran into something I thought I'd left behind in New York: problems with the manager.

Vic Power, who'd had a hard time getting along with some managers himself when he played for a number of teams in the American League, was the manager at Caguas that winter. Vic had been a great star as a kid in the Puerto Rican League, so he was a hero down there. Vic seemed to resent the non-Latin major-league players on the team. Maybe he still remembered his resentment when he was a young native player, unhappy about the guys coming down from the States and taking some of the play away from him. I can understand that. But a manager shouldn't let his own hangups interfere with the way he does his job. Vic Power had.

He seemed to want to set an example for the young fellows on the Caguas team by riding some of the more experienced players. He would constantly criticize the major-leaguers, whether we deserved it or not, and he always tried to make us the goats. We weren't about to take that sort of treatment. After all, we were down there out of choice, not necessity.

You could, with an effort, overlook Power's rages and scolding. But when he began inviting players off the team bus to fight, then it was something else. I didn't want to be a part of that sort of thing. And I believe Power sensed that I was at least one man who wasn't about to let himself be pushed around.

About that time I developed shin splints, an injury that you can pick up from running on hard ground. My legs kept feeling worse and worse, and one day I couldn't make it to the ball park. Ted Savage, an outfielder who was with the Cubs then, saw me before he left for the game, and I asked him to tell Power and the general manager, a man named Dr. Buonomo, that I wouldn't be able to make it. They both knew that I'd been hurting.

Savage told Power I wouldn't be at the park that day. But later Power pretended that he'd never heard a word from me. He told the press that Cleon Jones had jumped the club and gone back to the States, but I was in Caguas, and Power knew it. The next day I went to Buonomo and said, "Doctor, I can't play for this man. I want to leave. If and when he leaves, I'll be happy to come back and play." The general manager said he'd received other complaints about the way Power was handling the team. He said some players who were native Puerto Ricans, guys like Jose Pagan of the Giants and Felix Millan of the Braves, who'd never complained about anything down there before, had already spoken to him about the kind of stuff Power had been pulling on us.

Dr. Buonomo said he knew I'd been bum-rapped and asked me to stay around and see what happened. He hinted that Power was through. So I stayed a week. Power was still the manager. I went back to Dr. Buonomo and told him, "I'm heading out, but you know where to reach me the day Power leaves." I went back to Plateau. In less than two weeks the call came. Power had been fired, and they wanted me back because the team was a pennant contender. I returned to Caguas, hit .375, and helped the team win the Puerto Rican championship.

So I was in good shape, physically and mentally, for spring

training in 1968. Over the winter the Mets had hired Gil Hodges to replace Westrum. I knew that Hodges had done a good job managing the Washington Senators and that he'd been a big star on the Robinson-Campanella Dodger teams in Brooklyn. But I didn't know Gil personally, nor did I know the coaches he'd brought from Washington—Rube Walker, Eddie Yost, and Joe Pignatano. (Yogi Berra was the only one of Westrum's coaches who stayed with the team.) But I wasn't concerned about the manager or the coaches. I was concerned about Cleon Jones. I knew I could do the job, and I wanted to prove it.

I liked Gil right away. He was a leader, and he presented himself that way from the very beginning. I don't remember Gil's exact words, but I do remember that first team meeting in the spring of 1968. The manager's opening remarks don't change much from team to team and year to year—a little pep talk, a schedule of what the players are supposed to do to get into shape. It was more how Gil talked than what he said that made him impressive. There's an old saying about respect. It has to be commanded, not demanded. And Hodges commanded it.

Actually, getting into playing shape was going to be no problem for me. It never has been. In 1967 I'd stayed in New York for most of the winter and fattened up to about 215 pounds. When I got back to Mobile, I started working out, Angela cut me off at the table, and I was down to 191 in a month. Later, I got to thinking that maybe I'd worked myself too hard too early. Now, in 1968, I was reporting in at 192, but it was a weight I'd maintained throughout the off-season.

During the first week of training Hodges called me aside and spoke to me. What he said was familiar, too familiar, but how he said it was a change for the better. Gil said that for a while I would be platooned with Art Shamsky in left field, me against left-handers and Shamsky against right-handers. Gil said he knew I'd had a good rookie year and that I was capable of being an everyday player, but he said he didn't know our personnel well enough, and by platooning us he'd find out about me and Shamsky at the same time. I could see his point, and I liked the

way he put it. I didn't have to read about his plans for me in
the papers.

Art Shamsky was just one of a number of new faces in our
camp in the spring of 1968. He came to us from the Reds in
a trade for Bob Johnson, a thirty-two-year-old infielder. Art
was twenty-seven, and he'd once hit four home runs in a row.
It was a trade for a younger player, and Hodges made it clear
he was interested in building that way.

The very first move Gil made showed that. He sent Tommy
Davis and Jack Fisher, both twenty-nine years old, to the Chicago White Sox for my old County High teammate, Tommie
Agee, and a utility infielder named Al Weis. Agee, who'd been
traded from the Indians to the White Sox in 1965, was only
twenty-five. He'd had a bad season (.234) in 1967, but the year
before, he was the American League's rookie of the year. And
he promised to be the first legitimate center fielder the Mets
had ever had.

But where the club had picked up the most strength was in
the pitching staff. In 1967, as a rookie, Tom Seaver had won
sixteen games, and now two other guys in camp looked like
versions of Seaver—a right-hander named Nolan Ryan and a
left-hander named Jerry Koosman.

Before spring training I'd heard a lot about Ryan. He came
up at the end of the 1966 season and pitched in two games. That
was enough for anyone to recognize his promise. But in 1967
he hurt his arm and lost almost an entire season.

In 1968 he came back throwing bullets. His fast ball moved.
He needed schooling and confidence, but he had the kind of
arm that just doesn't come along very often. A lot of people
seemed surprised when he came up with a great World Series
game against the Orioles in 1969, but I wasn't. The only time
Nolan surprises me is when he doesn't overpower the other
team. I have a feeling that he'll come into his own now. You
have to remember that at the start of the 1969 season Nolan
had just turned twenty-two. Some pitchers don't walk into their
first major-league camp until they're twenty-three.

Koosman was twenty-four when he joined us in 1968 after
spending two years in the Army. I didn't know much about

Jerry, but over the winter in Mobile, Tommie Aaron, Hank's brother, touted me on him. Tommie had played in the International League in 1967, when Koosman was on our Jacksonville farm team. "He's got good stuff," Tommie told me. It was no lie.

So going into the 1968 season we had some pluses. We were young, and yet, for our ages, we were experienced. Ryan was twenty-one; Boswell, a rookie second baseman, was twenty-two; Swoboda, Kranepool, and Seaver were twenty-three; Bud Harrelson, a proven shortstop, and Koosman were twenty-four; Agee, Jerry Grote, and myself were twenty-five. We had at least one other thing going for us: We weren't losers, and we didn't want to become losers just because our shirts had "Mets" written across the front.

Not one of us was out of high school when Marvelous Marv Throneberry and the other Mets were losing a hundred and twenty games and becoming the clowns of baseball. We didn't want to hear that stuff. We wanted to win, and we were ready to do what it took to become winners. I think if there was one man responsible for that feeling, it was Hodges. It's very hard to look at Gil and think of him as a man who'd manage a crew of clowns.

Spring training in 1968 was longer than it usually is because we were scheduled to open the season against the Giants and Dodgers on the West Coast. Usually, even if you're opening away from home, you like to check in just before the season starts. You can get settled in the clubhouse, move your family into your summer home, and acclimate yourself to your home park. But we didn't do that in 1968 because it would have been silly to fly up to New York one day and go 3,000 miles across the country to start the season the next day.

Instead, we moved from Florida to California in hops, playing our final few exhibition games along the way. In Palm Beach, California, two days before the season was supposed to start, Dr. Martin Luther King, Jr., was murdered in Memphis, Tennessee.

I don't want to go into what Dr. King meant to us. A lot of men have expressed that better than I could. But I do know that his death affected all of us, white and black. Eddie Charles, a deeply religious man, was upset, but no more upset, say, than Ron Swoboda, who was raised in Baltimore when it was a Jim Crow town. Before the baseball commissioner ordered all the opening games canceled, we told Gil Hodges and Johnny Murphy, the general manager, that we wouldn't take the field against the Giants until after Dr. King's funeral. It was out of respect for him and for ourselves. The Mets have never been split along black and white lines, the way you hear some teams are.

The season started on a Wednesday afternoon in the wind at Candlestick Park. Since Juan Marichal, the Giants' great right-hander, was pitching Opening Day, I sat on the bench and Art Shamsky played. We lost a tough game (we'd never won an opener), but we won the next day in Los Angeles on a 4–0 shut-out by Jerry Koosman. The next night Don Cardwell, who always seems to lose well-pitched games, was beaten by Don Drysdale 1–0. After that we headed for Houston. The Astro-dome is a terrible place to play a baseball game, especially for the Mets, because we usually lose there. But this time we came in on a Sunday, and Nolan Ryan shut the Astros out 4–0. We had one more game, Monday night, and then we were flying home after seven weeks on the road. We were supposed to leave for the airport right after the game, and we did. Unfortunately, the game lasted twenty-four innings.

Tom Seaver started for us and pitched ten shutout innings. Eventually, however, we lost 1–0. It wasn't the best way to go home. I hadn't started the game, because Houston had a right-hander on the mound, but I went in for defensive purposes in the eighth inning—and wound up playing sixteen innings, almost two full games.

The twenty-four-inning game was probably toughest on Agee. He'd had only a fair spring training, but Gil stuck with him, and in the first four games of the season Tommie had a couple of key hits and a few good fielding plays to his credit. Unfortunately, in the twenty-four-inning game he went zero for ten. You expect to have some bad nights at the plate, when you're not swinging well or, occasionally, the pitcher's just too good. But if a pitcher's doing that well, you usually get only three, or at the most four, swings against him. But zero for ten, that's three bad games in one, and it can set a man thinking.

Starting with that night in Houston, Tommie went thirty-four times at bat without a hit, tying a Met record. It was the beginning of an awful season for Tommie, worse even than the season I'd experienced the year before. I kept telling him to relax, and so did Gil and the coaches. The fans were great, too. They refused to get down on him.

But it was awful for Tommie. In a situation like that a man who knows he's better than he has shown gets the feeling that any time he'll snap out of it. All he has to do is put a couple of hits together, and he'll be right there. But he begins trying to force things, starts doubting himself. A hitter like Tommie, a good hitter in a terrible slump, will walk up to the plate saying, "I'm going to hit the first pitch." He's overanxious. Another time he'll decide to wait the pitcher out, and he'll watch a curve go by him, right across the plate. Whatever he does is wrong.

In Tommie's case, he did break out of it briefly, but just when he seemed to hit a groove, he was hurt in Pittsburgh, missed a few games, and had to start all over again. Actually, Tommie's Met career began with the worst kind of injury a hitter can get. In his very first time up in our 1968 exhibition opener against the Cardinals at Al Lang Field in St. Petersburg, he was beaned by a pitch from Bob Gibson. Tommie went to the hospital for observation and was out and playing again in a few days, but there can be aftereffects from a beaning. A baseball thrown with the speed of a Gibson or a Ryan can kill a man. Every player knows that.

After a man is beaned, there's a chance that he'll come back ball-shy. And that's sudden death for a hitter. You're dealing with instant reaction, and any loss in a hitter's aggressiveness is an edge for the pitcher. If the pitchers discover that a hitter is shying away from inside pitches, the man might as well find another job. He's through.

I knew that Tommie wasn't bailing out at the plate. I saw him up there; I talked to him every day. Hodges knew it, too. And give Gil a lot of credit. Tommie was under .200 into Sep-

tember, and Gil still didn't give up. And finally, in the closing
weeks of 1968, Agee found his groove again. He wound up hitting .217, and he seemed more sure of himself in the field and
on the bases. All he talked about to me was next year.

Agee wasn't the only one having trouble hitting in the spring
of 1968. I was, too. Through April and most of May I played
only against left-handers and hit about .200. Then, late in May,
Gil started me against two right-handers in Atlanta, Phil Niekro and Ron Reed, and then another in Pittsburgh, Jim Bun-
ning. I was playing every day, and my average picked up. It
wasn't a coincidence. It's hard for me to platoon. I know every
hitter says he'd rather play all the time, but with some of us it's
a necessity. Our style of hitting requires a kind of rhythm that
is lost with inactivity. There are some fellows who can come off
the bench and hit well, but I'm not one of them. I have to keep
hitting and know what I'm doing up there at the plate to keep
myself together.

At the start of June I hit in eleven straight games—with
power, too. At the end of the month my average was up to .280,
and I had nine homers. But I wasn't about to go homer-crazy.
I'd learned that lesson. I was just concentrating on meeting the
ball. I was relaxed. There were two things I knew when I woke
up each morning that I'd never known in my earlier career as
a Met. I knew that I'd be in the lineup and we'd be in the game.
With Seaver, Koosman, and Ryan, we had the beginning of a
pitching staff that was going to become the best in all of baseball. We weren't there yet. But we were playing better, looking
better, and thinking better.

As the summer of 1968 wore on, we faded and eventually
wound up ninth. We won seventy-three games, more than ever
before, and we were more respectable as a team. But we were
still ninth out of ten teams. Now you can look back and say it
was a building year. But every second-division team calls those
seasons building years. When you're a winner, you're a winner.
When you're a loser, you're building.

The truth is we didn't come on stronger in 1968 because our

pitching suffered a couple of setbacks, and our hitting . . . well, our hitting just wasn't there.

Ryan was the biggest pitching disappointment. Early in the year he began developing blisters on his right hand. He had to come out of a couple of games, and he walked around soaking the hand in pickle brine, trying to toughen the skin. The hand cost him work, and that hurt more than the blisters, because Nolan needed experience to put the great fast ball to use. He had to develop backup pitches for the days when his fast ball wasn't working. Word got around the league to wait Ryan out. The fast ball was so live, it had so much action, that it wasn't a consistent strike pitch. After giving up a couple of walks, Ryan would go to his curve and off-speed pitches. They were only mediocre, and the hitters zeroed in.

But even with Ryan ineffective, our pitching was right up there. Our staff compiled the fourth-best earned-run average in the National League. And Koosman and Seaver won 35 games between them, behind only three National League pairs—Marichal and Gaylord Perry of the Giants (42), Gibson and Nelson Briles of the Cardinals (41), and Ferguson Jenkins and Bill Hands of the Cubs (36). No, we weren't ninth because of our pitching.

The hitting was awful, just awful. Our team batting average was .228, worst in the league. I hit .297, and Grote, who had an outstanding year both at the plate and behind it, was next at .282. Behind us, Eddie Charles had a .276 average and Ken Boswell a .261, but both as part-time players. None of the other regulars was over .242.

It wasn't an accident that a lot of players on one team seem to have good years and bad years together. A hitter depends on the rest of the lineup. If there are good hitters around you, the pitcher can't afford to walk you. He has to make you hit the ball. On the other hand, if you're the only man on the team hitting the ball well, the pitcher can pitch around you. It's a psychological advantage for him in two ways. First, he actually doesn't mind walking you. If it isn't a crucial moment in the game, he knows he'd rather take his chances with the guy on deck who's hitting 60 points lower than you are. Second, the pitcher knows that you are aware of all this and that you're going up there to hit, not walk. You're more likely to bite at a bad pitch.

But in a sense I felt that situation helped me as a hitter. It helped me gain confidence, knowing that I was able to do well in spite of this. And it taught me to discipline myself as a hitter. That's the most important thing a hitter has to learn, discipline.

I wasn't the only Met who gained confidence in 1968. When we started to slide, the attitude wasn't what it had been in all the other years. Nobody said, "Oh, well, we're the Mets. We're the clowns. We're supposed to lose." Instead, when we lost, we lost hard. And we kept looking forward to next year. Agee, for one, was always saying, "I'm going to hit good next season." That was the kind of talk you heard all over the clubhouse as early as August, 1968.

We didn't want to finish last, but we knew we weren't going to finish in the first division. So we concentrated on making the year count for us in other ways, as players. We watched, listened, and learned. The coaching staff was good, always ready with instruction or advice but never giving it just to show somebody up. Good teams feel pressure. They have to win or fall back. Bad teams feel a different sort of pressure. They have to improve or give up. We weren't winning yet, but we knew we were improving, and we were working at it.

We finished ninth, just three games out of seventh, and everyone said we had done well "for the Mets." But we felt, after 1968, that we had it in us to do well, period.

I was personally sky high. I hit only five homers in the second half of the season, to finish with fourteen, but nobody seemed to mind. The manager and the coaches had given us plenty of advice, but none of it was the stuff about pulling the ball.

Once I slumped a little because I stopped waiting on the pitches. Yogi Berra spotted it and quietly drew my attention to it. Yogi didn't broadcast it. And when I got a couple of hits the next day, he didn't go around bragging about how much he had helped. It was his job, and he just wanted to do it. That was the secret, from the manager and the coaches on down. Every man did his job. We were getting closer together as a team.

My .297 average was the seventh best in the major leagues.

Six hundred men in the majors, and I was the seventh-best hitter.

I'd wanted to hit .300. That's sort of a magic number in baseball. I had 509 official times at bat and 151 hits. I needed 153 to go over .300. Just two more hits, I thought, and of course I could think of a hundred ways I might've gotten them. But I didn't brood about it. I had too much to be happy about. And besides, I was already concentrating on 1969. There were a few business opportunities for me that winter in New York, but I told Angela that those would wait. We were going home to Alabama to relax and get ready for the next season. In a way I guess you could say the 1969 season started for me the day we said our good-byes in New York in October, 1968, and flew home.

But there was something else for all of us to think about when the season ended. Something serious. Gil Hodges was lying in a hospital in Atlanta. A week before, he'd pitched some batting practice and then complained of chest pains. That night we found out that he'd suffered a heart attack. None of us wanted to believe it because Gil was about as strong and healthy a man as you'd ever want to meet. But after the shock eased, I don't think any of us doubted for a second that he would be back in sixty-nine.

Maybe that was naïve, because after all, a lot of very healthy people get sick in a hurry. But you have to know Gil Hodges— as a person and a manager—to realize how strong-willed he is. He's the finest manager I've ever had in baseball. There was one time in 1969 when Hodges would let me down, but you can't judge a man on one move. He expects the best you can give, just as he gave when he played ball, and in October, 1968, there was no doubt in my mind that he would be out of the hospital and into a uniform by the spring of 1969. He was.

When I got home in the fall of 1968, the air still smelled from the paper mills, and the old shacks were another year older. But somehow Plateau looked different to me. I'd made it through all the bad things about Plateau, and now I could enjoy the good ones.

When I say that I wanted to relax, I want to make it clear that I mean *relax*. I may be a good outfielder and an excellent hitter, but if I'm anything, I'm an outstanding relaxer. The trouble with most people in the cities up North is that they never learn the meaning of the word. They're moving from the day they're born to the day they die, and after a while they're moving whether they have to or not. It's like a reflex action. You take a look at a resort place like Miami Beach or Las Vegas and you'll see what I mean. Those people are even moving on their vacations. They run around in circles.

Las Vegas. Now there's a place that can make you wonder what the world is all about. The Mets made a couple of stops in Vegas my first couple of years when we had days off on the way to California or on the way back. We played the slot machines, caught a couple of shows, and, either that night or the next morning, caught another plane out of town.

But in November, 1969, Angela and I would spend seventeen days in Las Vegas. We had won the World Series, and we had many offers, some of them utterly ridiculous. The most ridiculous of all was something that Frank Scott, who promotes business opportunities for players, came up with. Scott got Phil Foster, the comedian, to go along with the idea of taking a number of us to Vegas and putting an act together. It was so ridiculous that seven of us—Tommie Agee, Donn Clendenon, Art Shamsky, Eddie Kranepool, Tom Seaver, Jerry Koosman, and I—agreed to do it. They were giving us $10,000 each plus a free vacation to sing and crack jokes for two weeks at Caesar's Palace.

Angela and I left Anja with her mother and took off for Nevada. We were out there for a couple of days when we decided we'd made one mistake. Anja was always asking for us, and Angela's mother told us she was upset all the time. And we missed her, too. So Angela got on another plane, went back to Mobile, and brought Anja back to Las Vegas. Maybe my daughter doesn't need all the things I needed when I was young, but she does need love. And Angela and I discovered in those first couple of days that we need to give it to her. I was smiling so wide when the two of them walked off the plane that the other people must have figured I'd just hit the jackpot.

I didn't gamble in Vegas, actually. The day we got there to begin rehearsing, Phil Foster got us all together and told us that a couple of years before, some of the Dodgers had put together an act and gone to Vegas and come home without a dime. In fact, Phil said, some of them left Vegas owing money. "I'm not going to let that happen to you," he told us. We agreed to take $1,000 the first week and $1,000 the second and $8,000 when we were ready to leave. And none of us spent that much, because we were given a lot of free stuff. The greatest single expense I had for the whole time was the plane fare for Angela and Anja.

Everybody looks at those tables and thinks he can beat them, and almost nobody does. I decided I wasn't going to let that happen to me. I figured I was $10,000 ahead when I started, and that's where I wanted to stay. So I didn't play at all. Angela got to like the slot machines. And, funny thing, she actually won about $50. When we weren't rehearsing or onstage ourselves, we made the other shows. We were introduced all over town and met people like Buddy Hackett and Dean Martin. One show I think Tommie and I caught every night we were there was Redd Foxx's act over at the International. Foxx is one funny man.

As for our own act, my only worry was that people would expect too much. We knew we weren't performers, and we figured the customers would know that they weren't about to see Ray Charles or Frank Sinatra. We weren't ready for Broadway. Considering the talent we had, I thought we did pretty well. But we were like a rookie-league team playing in a major-league park, and everybody knew it. We didn't get any hecklers because I guess the hecklers figured it was like shooting fish in a barrel. But we didn't need hecklers. Usually, we did a pretty good job of heckling each other.

Before each performance, we knew what we were going to do, but somehow things never went according to plan. If we'd missed as many signs during the season as we missed cues i our two weeks at Caesar's Palace, we would've wound up i fifth place. And maybe the funniest guy up there was Seaver, because most fans wouldn't expect him to be the type who performs in nightclubs.

But Tom does everything well. He's the kind of man you'd want your kid to grow up to be like. Tom's a studious player, devoted to his profession, a loyal cat, trustworthy—everything a Boy Scout's supposed to be. In fact, we call him "Boy Scout." But with all that, Tom's not stiff. He's a fun-loving guy, and he's the first guy to kid himself. Someone walked up to him in Vegas and started reeling off all the records he'd set, and Tom looked back at him and said, "Yeah, but you forgot one thing: I'm the only pitcher in the history of the Mets who's lost a ball game in the World Series."

Clendenon was another guy who seemed at ease onstage. Donn's usually with it, a together cat. He'd come to the Mets at just the right time and given us what we needed in terms of his professionalism on and off the field. He kept us loose. Donn had nicknames for everybody, not the nicknames you read about in the paper but his own personal nicknames. I was "Little Fat Fella." He was always joking, but usually when he got on someone, it was with a purpose. He knows his baseball, and he can help you. About the only time Donn got very serious all season was just after he'd joined us when he wasn't playing a lot. He wanted to play so badly, and he'd sit at his locker after a loss and talk about how much he knew he could help the club. His locker was next to Tommie's and mine, and we kept telling him he'd get the opportunity. But none of us had any way of knowing that Clendenon would drive away with the sports car they give the most valuable player in the World Series.

Another guy on the Vegas trip who seemed at home was Shamsky, who'd just opened a little club of his own in Rockland County, just above New York City. Art and I have great respect for each other as hitters, and we'd helped one another during the season. At times I'd notice that he was moving his hands around on the bat and I'd let him know—maybe I'd see it right in a ball game and tell him then, or maybe he'd go bad for a couple of days and I'd look for it. He always said that I hit better when I swung my rear out on my backswing, and if he thought I was too tight at the plate, he'd yell, "Get your ass out there, Jones!"

Art is Jewish, and that makes him very popular in New York, which has the largest Jewish population of any city in the world. But that also puts a lot more pressure on Shamsky than he'd have if he played elsewhere. In the middle of the pennant race he took a couple of days off for the Jewish holy days. Nobody in the clubhouse resented that. We were the type of team that learned to believe in each other. This was something Art felt he had to do, and when you've got to do something, you do it. We figured that it had been a tough decision for him and that once he took the time off, he was more apt to help the ball club when he got back. The way I looked at it was that the worst thing Art could've done was to play and be out there thinking that maybe he shouldn't be. We talked to each other a lot during the year, and I remember telling him at that time, "If you're playing—thinking, 'Why am I here? What's going to happen? What's going to be said?'—then you're not going to be in the right frame of mind to help the team, anyway."

So we called him Rabbi Shamsky and all that, but it was only in jest. Really, I think we respected him for what he did, and he respected himself.

Shamsky was pretty loose onstage. In fact, we all were. The show would start with a film Phil Foster put together that showed clips of one error after another, things all seven of us had done before 1969. On the film we ran into each other, lost pop-ups, kicked grounders, gave up home runs, struck out, did everything wrong. The funniest sequence was taken a couple of years ago. Kranepool was running a man down between first and second, and he ran right by the guy without tagging him out.

There must have been some New Yorkers in our audiences, because Kranepool was booed. Eddie's always been treated unfairly in New York, partly because he's stood up for what he believes in. All the players appreciate Krane for going out on a limb as our player representative in the negotiations with the owners. Recently, he's been one of the leaders in gathering support among the players for Curt Flood's lawsuit against baseball.

The owners have done a good job of convincing a lot of fans

that if Flood's suit wins and the reserve clause in our contracts is declared illegal, the game will be ruined. That's just not true. Football hasn't had our kind of reserve clause for years, and it's stronger than ever. A man ought to have some say about the team he plays for, especially a man who isn't playing much.

Those are the guys, you see, who would benefit if players were allowed to move from one team to another without being traded. A star player is happy where he is. He's well paid, and he has roots in the town where he plays, business connections, friendships. He doesn't want to take a chance of losing all that with a new team. So he won't jump from one team to another for $10,000 or $20,000 more. The guy who the reserve clause really hurts is the little guy, who can be held back by one team. Take a guy like Tommie Aaron, who has pretty good ability but never got a chance to show it with the Braves. A few years ago there were a couple of clubs that really wanted Tommie, but the Braves wouldn't let him go. I guess they didn't want to risk getting beat by a man named Aaron. Tommie had a chance to better himself and make more money, but the Braves wouldn't let him take it.

Somebody has to fight for rights like that, and a guy like Eddie Kranepool, who speaks his mind, is a pretty good fellow to have around. It bothers us when he's made the scapegoat by some people who disagree with him, but I think Eddie understands that we appreciate what he's doing and what he's done. A few years ago, before guys like Krane began speaking out, the teams could pay their young players as little as $7,500 a year. We were the select few, the few hundred guys out of all the thousands of ballplayers who tried for the major leagues, and some of us weren't even getting a salary we could live on.

A man ought to be able to earn enough money so that he can stop and enjoy himself once in a while. He ought to be able to wake up when he wants to in the morning and go to sleep at night without worrying that he might've missed something during the day. That's what *I* call a vacation.

In the winter of sixty-eight back in Plateau I did all that. I spent time with my family, went fishing a lot, and loafed through the first couple of months down there. I'm not a base-ball player there so much as I am a person. If I were to walk back into town high-hatting people because I'm a baseball player, nobody would believe it. They'd think I was kidding. They know me better than that.

The only thing I did that even remotely resembled work was some basketball officiating. I went back to County High and visited with my old coaches, Charles Rhodes and Curtis Horton, and I tried to help a couple of their better baseball prospects. You can't teach anyone experience, but I figured that if one or two of those kids could be pushed even a little in the right direction, they would be helped.

I stressed fundamentals. Kids don't want to be bothered with the basic things. I know I never did. And I played a couple of years as a professional before I realized how important funda-mentals were. We went over bunting and throwing to different bases from the outfield. And we stood around for hours and talked hitting.

When I wasn't coaching or just plain loafing, I was out fish-ing. You could offer to take me on a fishing trip anywhere in the world, and I'd tell you to buy me a ticket to Mobile. Some guys like deep-sea fishing. They hire a boat and go out after something to hang on a wall. That's not for me. I like to fish the way I fished when I was four years old, in the rivers and creeks and out among the bayous of the bay.

Those deep-sea fishermen have to have someone to steer the boat and someone to spot the fish. When I go fishing, I steer the boat, spot the fish, fish when I want to, and leave when I'm ready. And the fish end up over a fire, not on my wall. When I was young, I dreamed about having a boat and fishing when I pleased and having enough money to enjoy all the things about Plateau that in those days I could only have once in a while. Now that I could make that dream come true, I wasn't about to throw it away because I could afford something fancier.

The easy life agreed with me. By Christmas I'd put on about 20 pounds of agreement. But even that didn't bother me, be-cause it fit into my plans for 1969. I wanted to go into camp about a month away from playing shape. I figured that one of the reasons I always had trouble starting well up North was that I'd always reported to spring training in playing shape.

You get used to competing down in Florida against guys who are just easing their way into shape when you're there already. You can get caught off balance in April when everyone else starts playing for keeps. Now I'd decided I was going to do it their way and see what happened. In January I began working out, easily, with Amos Otis and Agee and Tommie Aaron, plus two of the kids from County, A. C. Mosley and Norman Hill, who were about to sign contracts.

The Mets sent me a contract in January with a nice salary increase. At the time, I knew that the Major League Baseball Players Association was advising us all not to sign because there was a hassle on a number of issues the association was trying to settle with the owners. But as much as I sympathized with the association, there were other pressures. A player starts getting paid by a team from the day he signs, and there were things we needed the money for. This was a good increase, and I hadn't been making the kind of cash that allowed me to sit back from September to March without a penny coming in.

The association was doing great work, trying to change things in the major-league system that had bothered all of us. Some of the bigger name players, who'd been pulling in good money for years and had excellent off-season jobs, could afford to sit back and wait it out. But I had to think of my family. "If the time ever comes that this thing develops into something more serious," I thought, "then I can always not report to the team until it's settled."

It may seem illogical for the rich guys to have been the ones to stick their necks out, when most of the contract provisions the association fought for involved pension money and mini-mum salaries—things a Mays or an Aaron had little interest in. But there were, and are, other issues. Some of them go all the way back to the day each of us walked into our first training camp.

In that first week you sign your "life" away—your picture, your signature—to a bubble gum company and a bat company and a glove company for less than $200. Then if you become a big star, all you get is a few more dollars. Of course, you don't have to sign, but as a nineteen-year-old kid, you do what they tell you to. It's a racket that the owners and these companies have going, and the association wants it stopped.

The major-league player is hurt in two ways. First, when he's played a year or two and would like to have a model glove sold in his name, it is up to the company. There were several companies who wanted to put out a Cleon Jones model for 1969, but the company I signed with seven years before, Spalding, had my name locked up. They didn't use it themselves, but they kept anyone else from using it. And a year later, when the name Cleon Jones could earn real money because of the season we had, I was still getting practically nothing at all from the bat company and the gum card company.

As things turned out, I never faced the problem of deciding whether to report or not. The players and owners reached agreement a few days before the regulars were scheduled to report for spring training, at the end of February.

The day I reported to the St. Petersburg training camp I weighed 207 pounds, 15 over my 1968 reporting weight.

Reporters found out about my weight and asked me about it. I explained that with the extra weight, I would work into shape a little slower, reaching a peak in time for the season.

The writers asked Hodges about it. I guess Gil didn't think my logic was something he wanted to endorse publicly. Of course, he didn't want to knock me for being out of shape, either. So Gil said, "If he wants to believe that'll help him, it's fine with me. But Cleon reported in at one ninety-nine last year, and he was two hundred yesterday. He's one pound heavier this year." And Hodges gave them a wink, which is really his secret weapon. So they wrote that I was only a pound over. Only Gil, myself, and the trainer knew that it was really 15 pounds. He'd given them a 14-pound wink.

7

Spring Hopes

We had a terrible spring training in 1969. There were several injuries, uneasiness about a possible trade, and general sloppiness in our play. On top of that, Gil's big experiment of the spring, an attempt at making a third baseman out of Amos Otis, fell through. Despite these problems, we felt good about going into the season because we knew we were the most talented Met team ever fielded.

The biggest problem was Jerry Koosman's arm trouble. Jerry had won nineteen games for us in 1968. You don't lose the kind of ability he'd shown us, not unless your arm gives out. And in March, 1969, it looked like Koosman's arm might have done just that. He developed tendonitis and could hardly throw a pitch all spring.

Then Art Shamsky, my old left-field rival, bent down playing a game of pepper on the sidelines one afternoon and couldn't straighten up. He wound up in traction, and we heard reports that he might never play again. Gil had his eye on Art for some outfield platooning and a strong left-handed bat off the bench. Even though Art had hit only .238 the year before, he did have 12 homers in 345 at-bats. The Mets were like "Brand X" in those battery commercials on TV. We had no power to spare.

There was also a third physical uncertainty. Bud Harrelson, our shortstop, had undergone a knee operation in the fall. A shortstop's knees are vital because of all the pivoting he must do on ground balls and relay throws. And in Bud's case any loss in speed would hurt double, because as a hitter he depends on his head and his legs to keep him in the majors. Bud was being very careful all spring. That wasn't a bad idea. But sometimes guys come out of knee operations and never stop being careful.

The trade talk involved the Atlanta Braves' Joe Torre. A powerful catcher and first baseman, Torre, who was twenty-seven, had spent his entire career with the Braves, first in Milwaukee and then in Atlanta. But he and the Braves' vice-president Paul Richards wound up as spokesmen on opposite sides of the Players Association hassle. As the negotiations continued, Richards and Torre publicly, and bitterly, criticized each other.

After the dispute was settled, Joe became a holdout and eventually asked to be traded. Richards announced that Joe would never play for the Braves again. The newspapermen covering the Mets were convinced that Torre, a Brooklyn boy, would be traded to us.

The late Johnny Murphy, our general manager, talked about a Torre trade with Richards for several days. It was no secret that the Braves wanted several Mets for Torre.

The names were flying all around camp. The word was that we'd offered them Eddie Kranepool, Nolan Ryan, J. C. Martin, and a utility infielder named Bob Heise. Richards had asked for Jerry Grote, our number-one catcher, instead of Martin, the second-stringer, and Murphy said no. Richards said okay, he'd take Otis instead of Heise. Murphy said no again, and around and around they went.

Meanwhile, all this wasn't lost on all these guys plus almost anyone else who might be thrown in. And even those of us who felt sure we wouldn't be traded had to feel a little insecure. You're about to get settled for the season. Everybody's getting accustomed to one another. And now two or three new men may be coming in.

In the clubhouse and on the field we tried to stay loose about the whole thing. One day, for example, we were playing pepper on the sidelines, and a ball was hit too hard. It almost smacked Seaver. "You're ready for a plane ticket to Atlanta," I shouted at the guy who missed the ball. Someone else yelled, "Take him off the untouchables list." Murphy had called all the players he'd decided not to trade "untouchables."

Everybody laughed, outwardly. I had a year of youth and 26 batting points on Torre. I figured I wouldn't be traded for him, even-up. But some of the others must have had to force their laughs. Nobody wants to be traded.

Nobody was. The Braves finally sent Torre to the Cardinals for Orlando Cepeda. And we went with what we had. There's an old saying in baseball: Sometimes the best trades are the ones you don't make.

The brightest hopes of our spring training were the rookies. Amos wasn't happy at third, but he started off hitting very well. Rod Gaspar, a switch-hitting outfielder with an unusual open stance at bat, had a quick bat and speed on the bases and in the field. And Wayne Garrett, a second baseman we'd drafted from the Braves, looked promising.

I tried to help our rookies. They were in their own world, and I tried to make them realize that it probably wouldn't be that easy for them once the season started. I'd learned that much from experience. The veterans don't put out in the exhibition games.

Because I'd known him in Mobile, I was closest to Amos. He had a good swing, and he'd been getting a few good hits. "Don't go out there expecting this to happen when the season starts," I told him after one good exhibition game. "When those fellows out there know they're working to earn food and clothing for their families, they get a little tougher. This is only spring training." Amos thought he was ready. He nodded and pretended that he knew what I was talking about, but I knew better. I'd been a rookie once.

The pitchers throw hard in Florida. But in spring training a veteran pitcher isn't concerned with winning or losing; he just wants to get his pitches down to find his groove. A hitter can go to spring training and just look for fast balls. He'll get them. I told Otis and Gaspar this. When the season started, they didn't hit very well. But that first year is the toughest, and I believe both of them will be fine hitters. Kansas City thought so much of Otis' potential that they gave up a proven third baseman, Joe Foy, for him after the 1969 season.

I was sorry to see Amos go, but I thought this was one trade that would help both teams. The Royals are building, and they'll give Otis a chance to play every day. Actually, Amos stopped hitting just before the 1969 season even began. He let his problems in the field affect his whole game, and he got down on himself and the Mets. He made a few bad plays at third and just decided he wasn't going to be a third baseman. Amos had the ability to play any position with practice.

The more a man matures, the more he realizes that he has to accept things that he doesn't agree with. You have to look at the overall picture. It's something I learned the hard way, so I know it well.

There was another experiment in spring training. Cleon Jones was playing some first base. Gil felt that he might want to platoon Kranepool. Ed Charles had played some first, but with Otis failing at third, Charles might be needed there. I was the only other right-handed hitter who could possibly play the position. I wasn't crazy about the idea, but if I could help the team by moving in from left field in some games, I was ready to try.

As it happened, I got to play first quite a bit in the opening months of the season before we acquired Donn Clendenon from the Expos. And it taught me something. You never appreciate the difficulties of a job until you try it. I figured first base was easy. You caught the pegs from the infield and made conversation with the runners. That's what I thought.

One of the biggest problems an outfielder has is staying in the game mentally, keeping alert for the three or four balls that will come his way in a nine-inning game. But at first base you have to watch every pitch, be alert every moment. At first, no matter what happens, you have to do something, be somewhere other than where you're playing when the pitch is made. You're going to the ball or to the bag or to a spot where you have to back up a throw, and with a runner on, you have to cover the base before and after each pitch whether it's hit or not.

The hardest thing for me to learn was staying out of the way.

Now that almost sounds silly, but it isn't. If the batter hits a fly
ball or line drive to the outfield, even if it looks like an easy out,
he's going to come chugging around first base, and the first baseman can't be in his way. If you just stand there and wait to see
what happens to the ball—wham! You're on your back, and the
runner is awarded an extra base because he had the right of way.
Not only does a first baseman have to be somewhere on every
play, but he also has to not be somewhere, too.

Most of us felt that we were the best Met team ever to come
out of Florida. We talked a lot about finishing "in the money,"
which meant among the first three of the new six-team Eastern
Division. I think if we had a goal, it was to finish second in the
East, behind the St. Louis Cardinals.

The Cardinals, the Pittsburgh Pirates, the Chicago Cubs, the
Philadelphia Phillies, and the new Montreal Expos were
grouped with us in the East. Cincinnati, Atlanta, Los Angeles,
San Francisco, Houston, and San Diego made up the Western
Division. At the end of the season the two division winners
would play for the pennant, and the second- and third-place
teams would split some cash, as the first five teams in the league
had when there were ten teams and one winner.

We figured we had as good a shot as anyone at second place.
We felt nobody was going to beat the Cardinals. They'd won
two straight pennants and then traded for Torre, Vada Pinson,
and Dave Giusti. They just looked too strong for anyone—Lou
Brock, Curt Flood, Pinson, Mike Shannon, Tim McCarver,
Julian Javier, and Dal Maxvill, with a pitching staff that in-
cluded Bob Gibson, Nelson Briles, Steve Carlton, and Ray
Washburn. But we felt we were at least as good as the four other
teams in the East. We'd seen the Phillies, the Pirates, and the
Expos in Florida, and we knew they all had problems. The Cubs
were training in Arizona, but we knew their personnel. If they
had a few more names than we did, they were giving us a lot
of years, and over a long season those extra years add up.

And we had one more thing in the spring that I haven't
mentioned. For the third year in a row, we had come up with
a rookie pitcher who looked like he could win right away. That
was Gary Gentry, a slender, tough-looking kid with a live fast

ball and unusual confidence for a rookie. If Koosman came around and nothing happened to Seaver, we could count on three of the hardest throwers in the league. Behind them, Don Cardwell would give us some experience; Ryan was still fast; Jim McAndrew, a young off-speed pitcher, was a year smarter; and Tug McGraw, a very likable guy who'd been knocking around our organization since 1964, seemed to be putting all his good pitches together for the first time in his career.

Most of the experts picked us for fourth or fifth when the season started, but with a few breaks we knew we could do better than that.

8

How to Be a Hit at Bat

We play 162 games a season, and traditionally, for the Mets, the first is the worst. Going into 1969, we'd lost seven opening games in seven years.

Opening Day is the day the bands play, the color guard runs up the flag, the mayor throws out the first pitch, and the Mets lose.

But on April 8, 1969, we were supposed to end all that at Shea Stadium. Our opponents were the Montreal Expos, and it was the first game in their history. Seaver had a bad day, but he wasn't alone. There wasn't a pitcher we used who could do the job, and we lost 11–10. Montreal's pitching, obviously, wasn't very strong, either. (We got fifteen hits, I got three.)

But we weren't ready to say, "Here we go again." I remember telling Angela on the way home, "You know, Montreal's got a good hitting ball club. That's all they drafted—guys who could hit, like Wills and Staub and Bailey and Mack Jones. We're going to come right back tomorrow. Hell, we scored ten runs today, and that's a good sign. There aren't too many teams in this league who are going to get eleven against our pitching staff." And there weren't. Our pitchers allowed as many as eleven runs only four times all season. That's not bad compared to the twenty-eight shutouts they pitched.

The next day we bounced back and won 9–5, and there were several things about that game that made us happy. We hit well, up and down the lineup, and when our starter, Jim McAndrew, had as much luck with the Expos as our pitchers had the day before, Hodges brought in Tug McGraw. McGraw gave up one run in more than six innings. When he tired, Hodges went for Nolan Ryan, who finished the game. McGraw and Ryan were going to be important all season. No team can win with only two or three pitchers, and these two guys always delivered when we were depending on it.

McGraw needed the good start. He'd come to spring training on a now-or-never basis. He'd been a Met since 1965 and made some history by becoming the first Met to beat Sandy Koufax (who'd won eighteen straight against New York). But Tug was too young and inexperienced to be a major-league pitcher that early, and he was one of several young throwers who'd passed me in the minors going the other way. Except for a few innings one September, Tug had spent three straight seasons in the minors trying to find himself. After a good spring in 1969, Gil decided to go with him.

I knew what Tug was made of before that. I felt a special feeling for him because he'd come in for the same sort of bad-mouthing that I had. Tug talked first and thought later. Meaningless things he said and did would be blown up by people who'd hear a little bit about something here, a little bit there, and maybe add a little bit of their own for good measure. Pretty soon Tug had the reputation for being wild and undisciplined, and it wasn't true.

I'd been burned early in my career for the opposite reason. I was too shy, and not really knowing what to say, a lot of times I just let things pass without saying anything. When writers and fans get a hunch about something, they can make a lot out of nothing before you know it. In Tug's case, he'd just laugh off those silly stories about his wildness, but people would assume that the stories were true. In my case, I'd just keep my mouth shut while Westrum was letting people think I was stupid, and it was easy for someone to say, "He's so stupid he never says anything."

On the third day of the season Agee hit two home runs, and Gary Gentry beat the Expos 4–2. In the bottom of the ninth inning Montreal loaded the bases with two out, and Cal Koonce came in to relieve Gentry. Don Bosch, another of the Mets the Expos had drafted, was the pinch hitter. Bosch hit a line drive right at Agee in center field, and the game was over. It was the kind of game the old Mets had to lose. But we weren't the old Mets.

We did lose our next three games to the Cardinals. But we were close in every game, and the Cardinals were the best team in baseball. When we lost to the Phillies 5–1 the next day, we'd lost four straight and fallen to 2–5. But we bounced back the next day to beat the Phils behind Gentry and Koonce. And when we lost two straight at Pittsburgh, we came back to beat the Cardinals twice in St. Louis. We weren't playing .500 baseball yet, but we were coming back, and that was going to be a Met strongpoint all year. We were to have two more four-game losing streaks and one five-game streak over the season. But nothing longer than that. You've got to have winning streaks to become contenders, but, just as important, you have to avoid losing streaks.

We went through the first two months of the season the way we'd gone through the first couple of weeks, winning some and losing some. Koosman wasn't himself yet, and we weren't hitting very well as a team. One man who did hit was named Jones. I wasn't close to .300; I was close to .400. From that opening series against the Expos, I was in the groove. I was doing the right things at the plate, thinking the right way. You get into a kind of frame of mind after a while when you go up to bat expecting to get your pitch and drive it. I was a better hitter, and I felt it.

Most hitters are asked again and again, "Who are the toughest pitchers you have to face?" A lot of us say, "All of them." It isn't a complete lie. The hardest man for me to hit is Bob Gibson. He gives me fits. You face Gibson on a night when he's at his best and you begin to think that the man who invented the game made a mistake, that he should have put the pitcher's rubber 80 feet or 100 feet away instead of 60 feet and 6 inches. He throws hard with control, which means that he's actually throwing strikes that are unhittable. A man who throws with Gibson's style, but thankfully isn't quite that good, is Bill Singer of the Dodgers. Hard throwers like Gibson and Singer are the toughest for anyone to hit. Another type of pitcher who's particularly tough for me is the good sinker-ball pitcher, a man like Frank Linzy of the Giants. Everything he throws is going down when it reaches the hitter. You don't strike out against a man like that, but you find yourself swinging under the ball and popping up or swinging over it and slamming the ball into the ground, turning your power into an easy out. Juan Marichal of the Giants is a great pitcher, but I've always had decent luck with Marichal. He comes at you with so many different pitches that you're off balance. But if you stay alert against Marichal, you stand a chance of getting a piece of them. There are times, in contrast, when I'm not going to get a decent shot at anything Gibson throws.

The fans sometimes don't appreciate how much goes into a single pitch. The pitcher stands out on the mound with the ball in his hand, and you're standing there cocking your bat. It happens maybe 250, 300 times each game within about two and a half hours. I've heard people call baseball a slow game. If you can appreciate what's going on out there, it's anything but slow.

The pitcher starts out knowing two things about the hitter. He knows from his personal experience what pitches work best. And he knows the team book. Each team has a book on every hitter in the league. It's not a real book (although some pitchers have those, too), but it's a combination of everybody's thoughts on how a hitter should be pitched. Before each series the entire team meets and discusses the opponent's hitters. In addition, each starting pitcher will get together with his catcher before a game and run down the lineup again. The team book is only a general guide, because no two pitchers have the same repertoire. For instance, if a man with a good curve ball says that he's had success getting me out on a curve, it won't help another pitcher on the same team who doesn't have much of a curve.

The book on me, generally, is "move the ball around and try to get him out inside." That is, they'll try to keep me off balance by coming inside with one pitch, outside with the next, high, then low, and so on. But at the key moment, when they expect

I'll be swinging, they try to throw their best pitch inside to jam me, make me hit it with the thin part of the bat.

But they don't really pitch me one way, because at times I've hit well against all types of pitches in all places. In order to be a good hitter you can't have a consistent weakness. If they find a spot where they can just come in there and stay in there and get you out, then you've had it. If you can't hit an inside pitch, for instance, then all you're going to see are inside pitches. You've just got to adjust. That's the secret of hitting in one word: adjust.

The quicker you're able to adjust, the better you're going to be. And if you can't make the adjustment as a hitter, you're lost. The books are full of them, guys who come up and tear hell out of the league once around, then flop. It isn't an accident. The pitchers have developed their book, and the word goes out. "Smith can't get around on a good inside fast ball." All Smith starts seeing is the inside fast ball.

Once you've learned to adjust to all types of pitches and pitchers, the trick is to be ready for them. That's the second adjustment. They might throw you all fast balls today and all curve balls tomorrow, and if you can't stay a step ahead of them, you won't be an accomplished hitter. Staying a step ahead does require some guessing.

Guessing is a part of the game. Everybody guesses, although there are hitters who insist they don't guess at the plate. But if you press them on what they do, it amounts to the same thing.

A hitter will stand up there looking for a fast ball. He'll say to himself, "If he comes in with a fast ball, I'm swinging. If it's a curve, I'm taking." Then he says later, "Oh, I didn't guess. I was just thinking fast ball up there." I personally don't see one bit of difference between "thinking" fast ball and "guessing" fast ball. You're still more prepared for one pitch than another. I've actually heard them say, "I don't guess, but I'll look for a certain pitch in a certain spot out there." That's like saying, "I don't lie, but sometimes I don't tell the truth."

Now that I've said everyone guesses, I ought to point out that it's really the only thing a hitter can do in the major leagues. He doesn't have a choice in the matter. You can't be prepared to hit Gibson's fast ball and be just as ready for his curve. You try to do that and you'll hit neither. Instead, you give something up in order to get an edge. If I stand up there completely dumb, then I'm going to be beaten by his fast ball and fooled by his curve. Instead, I concede one of them and completely convince myself that the other is coming. I still might not connect, but I've got everything possible going for me. And I haven't really lost anything in the process.

The more pitches a pitcher has, the greater are the odds in his favor. That's what makes a pitcher like Marichal tough. He's got three or four good pitches, each coming at a different speed, moving differently when it reaches home plate. With a pitcher like that, you have to guess in generalities. You're either looking for hard stuff or off-speed stuff.

Experience gives you ideas on what to expect, and you have to put those ideas to work. Really, when you stop to consider it, what does experience do for a hitter? It makes him a better guesser.

But there are two times when the guessing stops.

One is at a crucial point in the game, usually when a relief pitcher has just come in. Most accomplished relievers are one-pitch pitchers. Their team needs outs when they come in, and they're being paid to challenge you with that pitch. If Frank Linzy comes in for the Giants with two men on base and one out, I know I'm going to see all sinkers. He's going to try to get me to hit into a double play, and that's his double-play pitch. It's his best against my best.

The other time when you can't guess is after the pitcher gets two strikes on you. Then the hitter must give up some of his aggressiveness at the plate and become defensive. He must try to get a piece of the ball to keep from striking out. But even on two strikes I sometimes guess. It depends on the situation.

Where a strikeout can only hurt *me,* not the team, I'll stay loose with two strikes and risk the strikeout for another good swing. Let's say there are two men out and nobody's on base. I don't have to protect anyone but myself because there's no rally going, no man coming up behind me if I go down. Usually

I'll guess fast ball and give the man his strikeout if he comes in with a good curve.

In that case I'm taking the good gamble, because at least I have a 50-50 chance of one good swing (more than 50-50 actually, if I'm taking an educated guess). If I'm defensive up there, I'm really getting no more solid swings at all. And a little nubber isn't any better than a strikeout.

It is a lot different from the kind of baseball most of the fans played when they were kids, or most of the players, for that matter. You get a good pitcher against a good hitter, and if you're close enough to the field and can learn to tell a fast ball from a slider from a curve, then you can really enjoy this game within a game.

A ballplayer, of course, has to back up his thinking with action. A pitcher has to do more than say, "He's set up for an outside slider now." The man has to throw it with speed, movement, and control. And the hitter can't just stand there with the bat in his hands and say, "I'm going to be ready for his outside slider now." He's got to follow the flight of the pitch, stride into it, and make contact with a solid, level swing. Without good execution, all the thinking doesn't mean very much. That's why a pitcher like Gibson or our Tom Seaver can be so frustrating and so good. You know what's coming, you prepare yourself for it, and you're still beaten. And a Mantle or an Aaron can make it just as frustrating for the pitchers. They can turn a man's best pitch into a game-winning homer.

If adjustment is the key word for hitters, then control is the secret of pitching. The pitchers who can throw the ball over the plate where and when they want stay around even if they're not overpowering. They won't win twenty games, maybe, but how many pitchers do? And control doesn't only mean the ability to throw strikes. Almost every pitcher can throw a strike if he wants to. Control means throwing bad pitches which are just good enough to make the hitter swing and just bad enough to keep him from connecting. On these kinds of pitches, the hitter becomes a fish.

Hitters who hit for average, as I try to, have to discipline themselves not to hit pitches that are out of the strike zone. A batter must be the fisherman, not the fish.

A pitcher will start out throwing the ball one inch off the plate. It's only an inch. You swing, maybe even hit the ball hard. Next time, the pitch is two inches off. You swing again. Now he's going to go farther away. The more you swing at bad pitches, the more of them you'll get. And the poorer you'll hit. Pretty soon you won't know the difference between a ball and a strike.

If the pitcher baits you into this kind of little game, he has to win. If the best place to hit a ball was four feet outside, then that's where they would have put the plate to begin with. You swing at bad pitches and you're playing his game. On the other hand, if you discipline yourself to swinging only at balls over the plate, then he has to come in with a good pitch or walk you.

Why give a man strikes he doesn't earn? It's hard enough to get a good shot at pitches in the strike zone. It's all part of the game. You go up there thinking for yourself and for him. And he's out there thinking both ways, too. For instance, if the batter in front of me had just walked on four pitches, I know the pitcher is having control problems and he might just want to throw a strike to regain his confidence, no matter what the cost. I'm on the offensive. But if the pitcher knows that I'm in a slump and he suspects I'm anxious to make contact, he may decide not to give me a good pitch until the count's 3–0. He has a hunch that I'll swing at a bad pitch. And even if I don't, he knows that if I do get a 3–0 count, I won't be swinging because the way I'm hitting at that time, I'll take a walk if it's only one pitch away. That's how complicated it gets. Hard to believe that a pitcher may throw three straight balls on purpose, isn't it? But it happens, and if the pitcher's confident enough and good enough, he can take his two "free" strikes after that and then have you swinging at a bad pitch again at 3–2.

That's a special situation, but generally you go up to the plate saying to yourself, "If *I* were pitching, what would I throw to try to get me out?" And again, the first rule is not to swing at a bad pitch. I know if I were a pitcher and the man at the plate was swinging at bad stuff, I wouldn't give him a good pitch to hit all day.

The pitcher starts out with the ball. He's in command out there. You have to concentrate before you can take the play away from him, before you can get the upper hand. The trick is to get to the point where you're not worrying about him—he's worrying about you. You're going to hit *your* pitch, not *his*. You're poised for your pitch, deciding whether to swing, taking your usual cut if you like the ball.

It is complicated. It doesn't come automatically. A baseball player is a professional. He has to study and concentrate, and the harder he works at it, the better he'll become. After you gain confidence and demonstrate some ability, the work doesn't stop, because the other team never stops thinking of ways to get you out. Then you pick up little things.

They can't make a .340 hitter out of a .220 hitter, but they can make the difference between a .297 year and a .340 year. What am I talking about? Well, for instance, there's the positioning of fielders.

When I first came up to the majors, I hit a lot to the opposite field. The outfielders and infielders began playing me toward right field, and the pitchers pitched me outside. I might get good wood on the ball and drill it to right center—where the center fielder would be standing, as if by magic, waiting to catch the ball. You tell yourself it's just tough luck at first, that you're unfortunate enough to be hitting the ball right at people. But when it keeps happening, you realize there's more to it than that.

I worked on pulling an outside pitch. I got so I could whip my bat out quicker and ride the pitch to left. If I guessed an outside pitch was coming, I'd do that, and suddenly my shots were dropping between the outfielders. Teams aren't stupid. If they get burned a few times, they change their strategy. Before a game the pitcher might have told his center fielder, "I'm going to put it out over the plate for Jones, so you shade him to right center." Then in the game I'd get my bat out quicker, pull the ball into left center, and wind up with a double or triple. It doesn't take many of those to make the fielders honest. I was challenged. I adjusted. Now they play me straight away.

Early in the 1969 season, when I was hitting around .400, people kept asking me whether I thought there would ever be another .400 hitter or, even worse, whether I thought I could hit .400. "I want to hit .300," I told them. "Everything over that is gravy."

There are so many things working against you as a hitter. You don't realize how many until you get up there among the leaders.

The last man to hit .400 was Ted Williams, and he did it in 1941. Things have changed in thirty years, and even if another man with Williams' ability came along, I don't think he could hit .400 today. First of all, the infields are allowed to grow higher now; the turf is richer and thicker. A high-average hitter is going to have to be someone with my style, a singles and doubles man who doesn't take the big swing, and he's going to have to put a lot of ground balls through the infield. The high grass slows the grounders up just enough for infielders to reach them. Once in a while it will give you a leg hit on a very slow roller, but if you hit a lot of slow rollers, you're probably closer to .200 than .400. Mostly, the grass takes hits away.

The infield grass, though, is the least of your problems. The greatest problem, as usual, is the pitching. If you're that hot, the pitcher will begin to pitch around you. The pitcher is just not going to let you beat him if you've got a hot bat. They'd rather walk you and try their luck with the man coming up next.

When that happens, you begin to get impatient, which is half the reason the pitchers do it. You're hitting well, and in order to stay in the groove you know you've got to swing the bat. If you walk four times in one game, you have the same problem in keeping your rhythm and timing together as you'd have if you stayed in the dugout and never got to play.

The alternative is to start swinging at what they're throwing you—bad pitches. And if you start swinging at bad pitches, you're going to come up against the kind of problems I've already described.

I know I'm making life seem awfully tough for a man hitting .375, but I've lived through it, and believe me, the pressure is there. It's especially rough on you when the team is involved. You know you're being paid to hit.

Now let us say we're at a crucial moment late in a close game. Maybe I've been patient my first three times up and wound up with two walks and a hit. Now we're one run up or down, there are a couple of runners on, and a man on deck is hitting 100 points lower than I am. I want to drive in some runs, or at least take a shot at it. I'm going to swing at anything near the plate, and the pitcher knows it. He has you in the hole before he throws a pitch. It kind of takes the bat out of your hands.

I could feel this happening throughout the spring and early summer of 1969. I knew that when the other team went over the Met lineup, the word would be, "Pitch around Jones." I knew because we did the same thing with hot hitters on other teams. And I knew because I stopped getting pitches to hit. One doubleheader, I walked five times. This was before we got Donn Clendenon and some of our other men started hitting the way they did in our stretch drive. The men behind me just weren't hitting, and the opposing pitchers didn't need a scouting report to know it. All they needed was a dime for the evening paper. The averages were right there.

Luckily, even through May, when we were under .500, we were getting enough key hits for a few pitchers to be burned because they wouldn't pitch to me. But it was still difficult for me, and I'm afraid I did get a little impatient up there. I started going after some bad pitches, and my average fell. It had to. Gil and the coaches recognized what was happening, and they helped me. As soon as I went after a bad pitch, I'd hear from Gil or Eddie Yost or Rube or Yogi.

When Ted Williams hit .406, he always said he'd take the walks and anything else the pitchers wanted to give away and make them pitch to him. Ted led the American League in walks for six years in a row, and he once had at least one walk in nineteen straight games. In fact there were years, before the qualification rule was changed from at-bats to plate appearance, when Ted didn't qualify for the batting title because he walked so much. As Casey Stengel likes to say, you can look it up. But while you're thumbing through that record book, be sure to note that Ted Williams hit for a lifetime average of .344, had 521 career home runs, and led the American League in hitting when he was forty years old.

I know that a lot of people criticized Ted because he might've driven in a few more runs for the Red Sox if he'd swung at an occasional bad pitch with men on, but I disagree. Sure, he could have won some games when he *started* to think that way, but it couldn't have lasted very long. He was a great hitter *because* of his phenomenal strike-zone judgment.

Look what happened to another guy in Boston in 1969, Carl Yastrzemski. Yaz is a fine all-round player, and he was one of the greatest hitters in the game. Then he started going for homers and runs batted in, and his average went down like some of my Wall Street stocks. In the long run, you can't help yourself or the club by swinging at bad balls.

Besides, the whole argument's wrong because you've got to have some other fellows in the lineup who can drive in runs. They can't be that bad or they wouldn't be in the major leagues. And if you *are* the only one who's capable of driving in runs, then it wouldn't matter anyway, because no team with just one hitter is going anywhere. No, I agree with Ted Williams 100 percent. It's tough enough getting your share of hits when the ball's over the plate.

A hitter can go for a bad pitch once, justifying it "because there's a man on and we're down a run and the man coming up behind me is hitting fifty points lower than I am." Then once becomes twice and ten times, and one morning you wake up, check the paper, and find out it isn't a problem anymore, because now the man behind you is hitting for a higher average than you are.

Another factor in hitting, but one that you have little control over, is the ball park. The background and general atmosphere of each park are different, and sometimes this requires adjustment. Of course, there's no place like home, and that goes double for Shea Stadium, our home field. I feel Shea is basically a hitter's park. There is enough area to make the outfielders play deep, and yet the fences are not so far away that they "rob" you of home runs.

The only time Shea becomes tough for a hitter is after the fifth inning of a day game, when the shadows from the stands obscure the ball for part of the distance it travels from the pitcher's hand to the plate.

But parks are becoming less of a factor because they are more uniform nowadays. As a line-drive hitter, I like a big park. That way, the outfielders must lay back to keep my doubles from becoming triples or inside-the-park homers. With small outfields and high walls they can play closer and take some singles away. But that kind of place is disappearing. When the Reds, Pirates, and Phillies move into their new stadiums, Wrigley Field in Chicago will be the only National League park built before 1959, and Wrigley Field has always been a great place for hitters.

The only stadium that bothers me is the Astrodome in Houston. I think the Astrodome is one of the reasons the Mets continue to have problems handling Houston. We lost all six games we played there in 1969 and five out of nine in 1968, including the horrible twenty-four-inning thing. I know I can't play my normal game at the Astrodome, and I know a lot of players who say the same thing. It isn't the idea of playing indoors that throws visiting players. It's the Astroturf.

You can't get a good start on artificial turf, and you can't stop as easily once you're under way. And when the ball is hit to the outfield, you have absolutely no idea of how it will bounce. Depending on the spin of the ball, it can take off, or hop up, or go left or right on you. You've got to lay back and let the ball play itself before you make a move, and it robs you of your aggressiveness. The Astros play under those conditions eighty-one times to six or nine times the rest of us do, and I believe it gives them a real advantage, both mentally and physically.

Before you get the pages too wet with your tears for all the .350 hitters in the history of baseball, I ought to point out that the pitchers don't only play their little fishing game with the top hitters. They'll pick their spots with every hitter. In the third game of the season, against the Expos, Agee hit those two home runs. Angela and I had him and Amos Otis over for dinner that night, and somewhere between hamhocks and greens and Angela's special two-homer banana pudding, I tried to talk to Tommie about the next game, against the Cardinals.

"Carlton reads the papers," I told Tommie. "He knows what you did today. He's going to try to make you take some bad swings before he's going to give you anything to hit. And he knows you want to keep swinging that bat." Tommie agreed. Then the next day he went zero for five. "I guess," he said after the game, "that's why you're a .350 hitter and I'm a .250 hitter." But of course that was no answer, and we both knew it. Months later, when Tommie was relaxed and certain of himself, things like that stopped happening.

A man can get home run fever easier than he can pick up the Asian flu. You hit a few out of the park and you want more. You don't stop to think the next day that when you hit those homers, you weren't consciously trying for them. You were just swinging well, and they came. Now you have home runs on your mind from the second you walk out there, and when you go up to the plate thinking home run, 99 percent of the time you aren't going to hit one. It's like a man who lucks into a straight to win a big poker pot and then spends the rest of the night throwing away decent hands to try filling inside straights.

You have to know the odds in poker and in hitting. It's great to have the power to pull the ball out of the park, but come to a game early enough to watch the pitchers hit in batting practice one day and you'll see guys with .090 averages calling for fast balls and belting them out of sight. Hitting is so much more than that.

9

Up from .500

On May 21, 1969, when Tom Seaver won his fifth straight game, our record was even at eighteen victories and eighteen defeats. It was the first time in the history of the Mets that we'd reached .500 later than the first week of the season.

Everyone except us made a fuss about reaching .500. We were looking beyond .500. We wanted to be among the leaders, and you don't get there playing just .500 ball.

We didn't have much time, however, to think about the difference between .500 and five games below it because a week later we were 18–23, the exact same record we'd had at the same stage of the 1968 season. And in 1968 we'd finished ninth.

Yet even at 18–23 we sensed that we were a much better team than the 1968 Mets. We hadn't been far behind in more than three of our first forty-one games. With a hit or two at the right moment, a lot of our losses might've been wins. We felt there was certainly room for more hitting. But our bats didn't come to life at Shea Stadium against San Diego the next night. It was a game that could easily have been our sixth straight defeat. We won 1–0, and it took us eleven innings to get that run. Jerry Koosman started for us. He'd pitched a few times in April, hurt his shoulder, then stayed out a month until one of the games in Houston, when he lost 5–1. The San Diego Padres started a twenty-year-old rookie, Clay Kirby.

We got a few hits off Kirby, but we flubbed every scoring chance. We were only in the game because Koosman looked as strong as he ever had. In the tenth inning Shamsky pinch-hit for Koosman and walked, but we didn't score. Koosman had struck out fifteen men in ten innings, and the score was still 0–0. Tug McGraw pitched the eleventh for us and continued the shutout. He picked up the win when we finally won in the eleventh inning. I led off the eleventh with a walk, and eventually we loaded the bases with one out, and Bud Harrelson lined a single to left.

We had the next day off, and Friday was Memorial Day, the first of a three-game series against the Giants. Holidays bring New Yorkers out, and any day Willie Mays comes to town is a holiday for the baseball fans. We (or at least Willie) drew more than 52,000 fans to Shea, and Tom Seaver was on the mound for the Mets. But we still weren't hitting. We'd scored eleven runs in six games and had been lucky to win one of them. Mike McCormick pitched a no-hitter against us for six innings and was leading 3–0 when Ron Swoboda hit a long homer in the seventh. It was our first hit. With one out in the eighth, Ron Gaspar hit another homer, and we were only down by one, 3–2. When Agee singled, Clyde King, the Giants' manager, brought Frank Linzy in to pitch to me. Those same old sinkers. But I timed one and got it through the infield, and Swoboda tied the game with another hit.

Linzy was still in the game, and Gil decided we'd pushed our luck sticking with right-handers. He sent Art Shamsky up to hit for Charles. Art's back had come around, and he'd put in a few good weeks getting in shape with our Tidewater farm club down in Virginia. Now he was back, giving Gil the kind of depth it takes to win games. This game, Art helped us without even coming to bat. When his name was announced, King came back out and brought in Joe Gibbon to pitch for Linzy.

You get Linzy out of a close game and you've done enough of a job. Gil called Shamsky back and put up a right-hander, Duffy Dyer, to hit against Gibbon. Dyer didn't hit the ball over the roof. He just got an infield single. It was enough. I scored from third, and with a good ninth-inning relief job from Ron Taylor, we'd won two in a row.

On Saturday we won again, 4–2, behind Gary Gentry with a

strong relief job from McGraw, and on Sunday we won again, 5–4, on four walks in the ninth inning. I'd come up in the ninth inning with Harrelson on third. I was hitting .364, leading the league. King ordered Joe Gibbon to walk me intentionally. That brought Amos Otis to the plate. I broke for second, trying to draw a throw so Harrelson could sneak home. But the Giants didn't bite. They let me take second. Then they walked Otis, unintentionally. Then they walked Swoboda, very unintentionally, and Buddy trotted home from third with the winning run. We'd won four in a row and overtaken the Cardinals to move into third place. That same Sunday the Cubs beat the Braves to stay nine games ahead of us. But we weren't thinking about the Cubs. Yet.

The next one was Monday night, the first of June, against the Dodgers at Shea. Jerry Koosman was trying to put two good starts back to back for us. I was on second base in the fourth inning when Jerry Grote hit a high pop-up. Ninety-nine times out of a hundred it's the third out. But you never stop running if you're on base with two out. You run as hard as you can for that hundredth time. I was one step away from the plate when I heard the roar. It was a windy night, and Grote's pop-up had gotten away from Bill Sudakis behind third base. We scored another run and won 2–1. We were back at .500, 23–23, and we weren't about to stop. Now the other guys were making the mistakes.

The next night Seaver was back. That's the way it is when you're going well. You turn around and there's your star pitcher ready for another outing. Kranepool gave us a run with a homer in the fourth inning. With two out in the fifth and Wayne Garrett on first, I hit a high fly fairly deep to right center. I glanced over my shoulder, rounding first, and saw Willie Davis and Andy Kosco collide. I wound up on third with a triple, and Garrett scored. A few seconds later Kranepool hit another one over the wall, and it was 4–0. We won 5–2, six in a row.

Now .500 was behind us for good.

Wednesday night Bill Singer pitched one of his great games, a two-hitter, and struck out ten. But it's a funny thing about winning streaks: They give you momentum. We had a guy named Jack DiLauro, just up from the minors, pitching for us. DiLauro has been kicking around for a long time, and he isn't a real strong pitcher. But on June 4 he went the same nine innings Singer did and allowed the same two hits. Tommie Agee walked in the fifteenth and scored the winning run on an error. Jack DiLauro, Tug McGraw, and Ron Taylor had shut the Dodgers out for fifteen innings, and we'd won seven in a row.

Friday night, in San Diego, we were tied 3–3 when I reached first with two out. The pitcher was a young reliever named Gary Ross. The Padres had drafted him from the Cubs. I studied him, took a lead, and when he went to the plate, I was off for second.

It's the percentage play, stealing with two out. It would take two hits to score you from first, and unless there's a .600 hitter at the plate, you stand a better chance of swiping second than he does of getting a hit. The best hitters in the game go three for ten. Even with them looking for you to steal, with enough speed and a decent jump you ought to steal safely at least six times in ten tries.

San Diego was playing the percentages, too. But those percentages seem to work a lot better for you when you're winning. The Padres walked Kranepool intentionally to get to Swoboda. Then Gil sent Shamsky up to hit for Swoboda, and Art lined a single to right, scoring me with the go-ahead run. Eight straight.

The San Diego starter on Saturday night was Johnny Podres, a left-hander who'd won a World Series for the Brooklyn Dodgers in 1955. But this was 1969. Podres' comeback was almost at an end. He'd pitched well a couple of times on sheer guts and cunning. The Mets had pitchers like that when I was coming up, pitchers like Warren Spahn and Bob Friend and Frank Lary, trying to keep themselves together for one or two more seasons.

But now we had guys like Koosman. Jerry pitched a five-hitter; we got twelve hits and won our ninth straight game 4–1.

Sunday we had Seaver going for us again. The Padres started Al Santorini, a right-hander who had been the last pitcher to beat us. Seaver's fast ball was blazing, but he wasn't getting his pitches where he wanted them to go. He struck out fourteen men in the first six innings, but the Padres scored twice, and the only hit we had was a single I'd gotten in the fifth.

A lot of fans think strikeouts are big things to a pitcher. But most pitchers, real good ones, will get their share of strikeouts without trying for them. In order to earn a strikeout, they have to throw five or six pitches. They'd rather have the hitters swinging into groundouts and pop-ups on the first or second pitch. I know that's the way both Seaver and Koosman feel, and that game was a good example of why.

We scored a run in the seventh on my second hit, but we were still down 2–1 in the eighth, and Seaver had thrown a lot of pitches. Gil had Gaspar hit for him with Ed Charles on first. Seaver could have bunted Eddie to second, but there's an old rule: On the road in the late innings you play to win. Hodges flashed the hit-and-run sign, and Gaspar hit the ball behind Charles to second base. In the statistics books it will always be an out, but hits and outs aren't all there is to good baseball. Charles, running, made second easily, Harrelson walked, Agee doubled in the tying run, and Rusty Garrett singled home the winner. We were headed for San Francisco with a ten-game winning streak.

The streak ended in San Francisco, but not before we'd won our eleventh 9–4. I hit a three-run homer, and Tommie drove in three more runs with two homers. They were calling us "the kids from Mobile." Cardwell pitched into the ninth, and Ron Taylor got the last two outs for his fourth save in the eleven games.

When it was over, we got whipped good and solid. We lost to Gaylord Perry 7–2. But we weren't upset after the game. It was almost the opposite. We came into the clubhouse and kidded ourselves about knowing that we had to lose at least once more before the season ended. I don't know if we'd proven to the rest of the league that we were for real, but I do know we'd proven it to ourselves.

We knew that the pitching was there and the defense was there (and that was something we didn't get credit for until the World Series). Defense isn't something that's good or bad on one or two sensational plays. You have to see a baseball team play every day to appreciate good defense. It means good positioning, solid execution, and few mistakes. Sure, the great plays help. But it's like a cornerback in football. His interceptions don't mean a thing if he can't stay with the pass receivers on every play.

The key area for defense is the middle of the field. And we had a strong middle. Grote, behind the plate, had a good arm. With Al Weis at second and Harrelson at short, we felt we had as fine a fielding second-base combination as there was, including Glenn Beckert and Don Kessinger of the Cubs. And in center field Agee was relaxed enough to do his thing. Hell, he'd been a great center fielder when he was eighteen years old.

After the loss to the Giants we were seven games out of first, and we felt the Cubs could be caught. We knew they weren't a fluky team. They were good. But they were older than we were, and there were reasons for us to think they'd get tired and tight before we would. They showed no signs of folding, but it was only the middle of June. Leo Durocher was playing seven of his men every day and working his pitchers harder than a man with a seven-game lead should. If you give a man an extra day's rest in June, he might win an extra game for you in September. By the middle of August it could begin to tell.

This sounds like hindsight. But I remember talking with Agee and Swoboda and some of the other guys about it the day our eleven-game streak ended. We'd won our games with fifteen or twenty players, different guys coming through every day. The contrast between us and the Cubs was obvious.

Three years before, in 1966, the Cubs had finished tenth, the first team in the history of baseball to finish below the Mets. But that was Durocher's first year as manager, and Leo was building something. He played kids—Kessinger, Beckert, Randy Hundley, the catcher. And he gave young pitchers like Ferguson Jenkins, Ken Holtzman, and Bill Hands a chance to pitch regularly.

It began paying off the next year when Chicago finished third. They were third again in 1968, after making a strong run at the Cardinals in the middle of the season, and in 1969 they were doing it all. Ernie Banks, Ron Santo, and Billy Williams had always been excellent major-leaguers, and now they had those other fine players to go with them. The one kid from 1966 who'd failed to make it was the center fielder, Adolfo Phillips, and Durocher had never really found another one, but the way the other Cubs were going, it didn't seem to matter.

When the Cubs finished behind the Mets in 1966, guys kidded Leo. He hadn't managed in more than ten years, and he had come back to be a loser. But Durocher had the right idea then. He told everyone, "Tenth place and second place are the same thing. They only pay off on one winner where I come from." And the Cubs in 1969 looked like he'd made them winners. They were even getting help from an unexpected source, a former Met. Jim Hickman, who'd even tried pitching for the Dodgers before he wound up in Chicago, was playing center field on a part-time basis and hitting a home run every time the Cubs seemed to need one.

But it was still only June, and except for their military commitments, the other seven men were playing every day. And in Chicago every day means every *day*. There are no lights at Wrigley Field. Ernie Banks likes to say that playing day ball for half the schedule has added years to his career, preserved his sight, and kept him out of the cold night air. But I think Ernie and Leo and the rest of the Cubs found out something about the summer sun in Chicago in 1969.

Night baseball may be tougher on your eyes, and if you don't watch yourself, you can catch cold. But day ball is tougher on your body, a lot tougher. That hot sun can drain you of your energy, day after day after day. You have to rest more often. And the one thing the Cubs couldn't afford to do, or at least the one thing Durocher thought they couldn't afford to do, was rest.

True, Chicago didn't start out with much of a bench. But the time for Leo to make more of what he had in the way of reserve strength was in the middle of the summer when he had that fat lead and everything was going well. That would've given twenty-five guys a sense of winning, instead of ten or twelve. It might have given the second-line players more confidence, and it definitely would have preserved the front-liners.

Instead, Durocher drained the team, like a jockey who whips a front-running horse out of the gate and never stops. Maybe Leo was afraid the Cards would wake up and make a run at him. I know he wasn't afraid of the Mets. He said so all summer long.

In June all this was just talk. We had to go out and do it, on the road as well as at home. We went into Los Angeles and lost two out of three to the Dodgers, then flew to Philadelphia and split four games with the Phillies. We'd won eight out of twelve on the road, and we were home for a four-game series against the Cardinals, only five and a half games out of first place.

A crowd of over 54,000 came out to watch us face Gibson on Friday night. We had Nolan Ryan going for us. In past years it didn't matter too much who the Mets pitched against Gibson. He'd had a 21–3 record against the Mets going into the 1969 season. But before the big crowd on June 20, we scored three runs in the first inning and one in the second and won it 4–3 with six innings from Ryan and three from Tug McGraw.

Gil was using Agee exclusively as a leadoff man by June. I would have rather seen Tommie hitting either before or after me, but there were some games when it was nice to have him leading off. This was one of them. Tommie led off against Gibson with a double. Ken Boswell got an infield hit, and Rusty Garrett walked after the Cards flubbed his pop foul. Bases loaded, none out. "He's got to come in to me, give me a pitch to hit," I thought. "The infield's back. They'll give up a run for a double play. He's going to come in with hard stuff, down. Ground-ball pitches." Sometimes you're better off playing at their strength. You try pulling a low fast ball over a wall and wind up with nothing. I guessed fast ball, met it head on and drove it through the middle, and we scored two runs. A few seconds later Shamsky followed with a sacrifice fly to make it 3–0. Boswell tripled in another run in the second, and we didn't need any more. We might have, but we didn't because in the first inning we threw Vada Pinson out at home. Pinson was on first with Joe Torre up and two out. Torre hit a hard line drive, over and away from me in left. Pinson, with two out, was running all the way. You had to think he'd score. But you also had to try to stop him.

On that kind of play you don't hesitate for a second. I caught up to the ball near the fence, turned, and fired to a spot. Harrelson's job is to be at that spot. He was there, caught the ball, and fired it home. Grote put the tag on Pinson, who must have been the most surprised man in the park.

We were surprising a lot of people, day by day. And that night at Shea Stadium we had a new face in the dugout. We'd picked up Donn Clendenon, a tall, powerful first baseman, in a trade with the Expos. Donn had hit twenty-eight homers for the Pirates in 1966, and he had a lifetime average of .280. They called him the Big Train. He's six feet four, and when he's hitting well, he must look like a right-handed McCovey to the pitchers.

Clendenon was thirty-four years old in June, and he'd played with some winners. He gave us experience and depth. Gil platooned him from the start, playing him against left-handers while Kranepool played against right-handers, and I know Donn resented it. He saw something big happening, and he wanted to be a big part of it. But Gil was able to keep him going at full speed that way and still get good use out of Kranepool, who's a better ballplayer than a lot of fans give him credit for. (The Mets gave him an $85,000 bonus to sign, and the fans expect him to hit .850.) Against left-handers, Donn usually hit right behind me. There were times when he tried a little too hard, and his big swing gave him more than a few strikeouts. But there were other times when he connected and won games for us. It took some pressure off me. I could take my walks with a clear conscience, and I could go for singles and doubles even if we needed a long ball because I knew we had three pretty fair cuts waiting on deck.

We won two of our next three from the Cardinals and took the first two games in the following series, against the Phillies. That made it twenty-one victories in twenty-six games and put us just four and a half games behind the Cubs. "At this rate," I told Agee, "we'll win the pennant by ten games." It wasn't a bad guess, but it didn't happen exactly the way I had in mind.

We lost the next four games before beating the Pirates behind Seaver 7–3. Tom's record was 12–3, and we weren't into July yet. But now there were lots of doubleheaders coming along. The schedule calls for 162 games in 178 days. With rainouts and travel days, you can't do it without doubleheaders. And doubleheaders meant that we weren't going to have Seaver and Koosman once every four games every time around. Our second-line pitchers would be used more, and even if they did well, they weren't going to be Seavers and Koosmans.

We went into St. Louis June 30 for a five-game series, four games on the schedule and one postponement from a rainout in April. We ripped them in the first game, 10–2, then lost both halves of a doubleheader the next day. Ryan and DiLauro were the losing pitchers. The Cubs were still winning. We'd slipped to seven and a half games out.

We had Koosman and Gentry ready for the last two in St. Louis and Seaver for our opener at Pittsburgh July 4. That, of course, was the first game of another doubleheader, our twenty-first and twenty-second games in eighteen days. We won all four of those games, but pitching didn't have everything to do with it. The scores were 6–4 and 8–1 in St. Louis and 11–6 and 9–2 in the doubleheader at Pittsburgh. And we didn't stop at four. It rained July 5, but on July 6 we beat Pittsburgh again, 8–7, and headed back to New York for a series against the Cubs. We were five games out, only three in the loss column.

Going into that three-game series against Chicago we had regained our momentum. Again, it's easy to spot the turning point now. That was the night after we'd lost the doubleheader in St. Louis, a hot Missouri Saturday night. It was so muggy the mosquitoes stayed inside. It was a tough night to have to go out and play nine innings. We had it even tougher. We played fourteen.

Koosman had a 4–0 lead into the eighth, when the heat got to him in a hurry. He walked three straight men. Gil brought in Ron Taylor, the veteran from Toronto who had saved us so often in the past two months. Vic Davalillo came up to pinch-hit and got a grand slammer. We were tied 4–4. We finally won in the fourteenth, 6–4, but not before Tug McGraw stranded nine men on base in six innings of tough, sudden-death relief pitching. Tug had given us six of the guttiest innings of his life.

We came alive after that long Saturday night and scored thirty-seven runs in our next four games. We even scored nine runs for Don Cardwell. We got thirty hits in the July 4 double-header at Pittsburgh. Al Weis, who wasn't supposed to hit his weight, went five for nine. Agee went five for ten with a homer. I went four for ten and moved into the National League batting lead with a .356 average. We didn't whisper it. We shouted it. "Bring on the Cubs!"

10

Kicked Out . . . and Pulled Out

Tuesday afternoon, July 9, was a beautiful day for the Mets and for baseball. There were 55,000 people in the stands, 20,000 of them kids who were in on the house. The Mets probably could have sold every one of those 20,000 seats, but each year our stadium manager, Jim Thompson, arranges for a number of games in which the team can donate tickets to youth groups. All this is done before the season even starts. I can just see Jim Thompson up in the offices at Shea now, looking over the schedule and saying, "Hmm, an afternoon game in July against the Cubs. We probably won't draw five thousand to that one. We'll give 'em twenty thousand seats."

Kids are the best baseball fans. They come early, yell all day, and never give up. The youngsters in the neighborhood where we live during the season tag along whenever I take Anja for a walk or go shopping or travel to and from Shea. Sometimes I do get tired of signing autographs, but I never get tired of talking to the kids. I know how I felt when I was young, what I'd have given to be close to a major-league baseball player for just five minutes.

I did meet Hank Aaron when he came back to give a talk at the high school, but by then I was a teen-ager. When I was younger, young enough to think baseball players were gods, there was no chance. I had to create make-believe heroes, like the fellows who played for our semipro team in Plateau and the players on the black barnstorming teams. And I never got the chance to be close to any of them.

I thought about that during batting practice that Tuesday afternoon. Every time one of us standing in the batting cage hit a ball toward the fence, there would be a loud, long roar from the upper deck where the kids were already sitting, more than an hour before the game. By the time we went out for fielding practice (the home team takes batting practice first and fielding practice last), the place was almost full. We had played before full houses many times before, but this was different. The papers were calling it the first crucial game ever played at Shea Stadium. There were so many writers and broadcasters on the field before the game that we couldn't throw the ball around in front of our dugout, as we usually did to loosen up, for fear of killing somebody.

When the Cubs came out for their practice, Billy Williams saw Angela sitting with Anja in her lap and walked over to say hello. She told him she was sorry, that all these years she'd been rooting for him to win the pennant with the Cubs and now she was there, with 55,000 other people, hoping he'd lose. Billy just laughed. "You'll get a chance to root for me in the World Series," he told her. Then they both laughed.

Inside, nobody was laughing. Both the Cubs and the Mets had been waiting for this series for several weeks. The proof was in the pitching. It's no accident that important pitchers are ready for big series. We were going with Koosman, Seaver, and Gentry against Ferguson Jenkins, Ken Holtzman, and Bill Hands.

Jenkins is a hard thrower, one of the best pitchers in baseball when his fast ball is moving. And that day it was moving. Koosman was not as sharp, but he was tough when he had to be. The score was 1–1 in the seventh. But Jenkins put himself ahead when he walked and scored on Beckert's hit. The Cubs made it 3–1 in the eighth on a home run by the ex-Met Jim Hickman.

The Cubs didn't score any more, but it really didn't seem like they had to. Jenkins was better than good. After a homer by Kranepool, he got eleven men in a row and went into the bottom of the ninth inning with a one-hitter.

Koosman was scheduled to lead off the ninth, so Hodges sent up Ken Boswell. It hadn't been much of a year for Bozzy. He'd made three errors in our opening game against the Expos. Then he got hurt. Now in July, in the first crucial game in the history of the Mets, Gil had decided to go with an infield of Garrett, Weis, and Pfeil at second, short, and third, even though Boswell was a better hitter than any of the others.

Boswell hit one in the air to center field. You just don't get much of a line on a fly ball at Shea because it goes up through the white shirts in those five decks of stands. To make things worse, by the ninth inning of a day game the sun isn't too much higher than the top deck. And still worse for the center fielder, on a ball hit right at a man there is no angle to judge. He must use every bit of experience he has to make what everybody in the park considers just a normal play. And Don Young, the Cubs' outfielder, was a rookie. At the crack of the ball against Bozzy's bat, Young stepped back. A moment later he realized that the ball was no more than a pop fly, but by then Young had committed himself. The ball plunked down on the grass between him and Beckert and Kessinger. Boswell had a double.

The crowd was alive. You could just feel the excitement. And we had three good swats at tying the game. Agee, Clendenon hitting for Bobby Pfeil, and me.

Tommie just missed pulling a ball inside third and down the left field line. Then he popped to the first baseman. But Clendenon hit a drive to deep left center. Young had been playing deep, and if the ball didn't hit the wall, he'd have a good shot at it. It tailed off, and Young grabbed it and slammed into the wall. The ball rolled out of his glove, and Boswell, who had been heading back to second base, reversed himself and made it to third. Clendenon pulled into second with a double. He was the tying run.

For a few seconds I wondered whether they'd walk me intentionally to try setting us up for a double play. But there's an old rule in baseball: Never walk the winning run. I decided Jenkins would pitch to me but try to get me to go after a bad ball. I also figured he'd lost some hop on his fast ball and he'd try to get me with breaking stuff. If I could just hit the ball through the infield, we were tied. That was all I wanted.

The first pitch was a slider, low. I was looking for an outside curve ball. That's what Jenkins came with next, but it stayed over the plate. He tried to do too much with it. I swung, and the first thought that came to my mind was that it had been too good a pitch to hit, too easy, and I'd pulled it too much. If I'd been swinging for the fences, that's exactly what would have happened. But I was following the rules, just meeting the ball. It went over third on a line and stayed fair, and I got a double, tying the game.

They walked Shamsky to try for a double play on Garrett. Rusty topped a grounder to second, and there was no chance for Beckert to get either Shamsky or me out. He threw Garrett out at first. I was at third base, 90 feet away from a win. Kranepool was coming up. I figured they'd walk him to load the bases with J. C. Martin up. But they pitched to Eddie, and Jenkins got two strikes on him. Kranepool was just protecting the plate, and Jenkins went outside, looking for the strikeout. He should've gotten it. But Kranepool threw his bat at the ball and blooped one over shortstop. I scored, but I could hardly believe it. Jenkins had a one-hitter into the ninth, and we'd beaten him with three fluke hits. I had a strange feeling that we might never lose another game. I was really hoping that some of the Cubs felt they might never win another one.

And for a while the next night, I believe the Cubs were wondering if they'd ever get another hit. Any time we have Tom Seaver going for us, we expect to win. He's our ace, our number-one stopper. Jenkins had been theirs, and we'd beaten him. So we were sky high going into Wednesday night's game, anyway. And Seaver had something extra on the ball, even for him. He couldn't seem to do anything wrong. Every pitch was just where he wanted it. He was perfect. Well, almost perfect, anyway.

We got a run off Ken Holtzman in the first inning and knocked him out with two more in the second. Meantime, Tom was mowing them down, inning after inning. When I hit a homer in the seventh to give us a 4–0 lead, almost nobody cared. Seaver was six outs away from a perfect game. The way Tom was pitching, whether we would win or lose had never been a serious question. The only thing was whether Seaver would pitch a perfect game.

We didn't say anything about it on the bench. Part of that is baseball superstition, but part of it is that there's nothing to say. You don't want to bother the pitcher. He knows what he's got going.

Out on the field, you want the next pitch hit right at you. The fielders are part of a perfect game, too, because any play that puts a man on base ends it. The pitcher will still have a no-hitter if there's an error, but his perfect game will be gone. But you don't think about errors; you think about outs. And once we had three or four runs in the bank, we thought only about preserving the perfect game for Tom.

Agee and I were looking over at each other on every pitch. By the seventh inning we were cheating, trying to be ready for the big play. We were playing much farther in for the hitters, giving them a better shot at an extra base hit in the hope that we would be able to take away a short sharp single. In a game like that you're riding every pitch home, ready to break one way or another. The pitch Jimmy Qualls hit with one out in the ninth inning was no different.

Qualls was playing center field that night, a left-handed hitter against Seaver, who, of course, is a right-hander. Qualls had pulled the ball twice earlier in the game, a long fly to Swoboda and a grounder to Clendenon. So Agee shaded him to right center field. In left, I had to protect the line. The way Seaver was pitching, you had to figure there was more chance of an accidental bloop to the opposite field than a solid hit. In the end Qualls did hit it to the opposite field, but his shot wasn't a blooper. He got a solid hit, a sinking line drive to left center. Tommie and I ran as fast as we could, but there was no way. It was a hit.

Tom got the next two men, and we won 4–0. It had been an emotional game. We were only three games behind the Cubs, with one more the next day, but there was a letdown. Maybe there had to be. We lost to the Cubs on Thursday 6–2, and on

Friday we were bombed by the Expos 11–4. It rained Saturday, and we watched the Cubs beat the Phillies on television 7–4. We were four and a half games behind again going into Sunday's doubleheader against the Expos, almost where we were before the two back-to-back victories over the Cubs early in the week. One thing a pennant contender learns in a hurry: They all count. You don't win games in your head. You win them, and lose them, on the field. For us, a game against Montreal had to be as important as a game against Chicago, because when it was over on October 2, all they'd be doing in the league office would be counting the wins. Nobody could tell us that some games counted more than others. And we didn't have the kind of power in our hitting that could break open most games, even against second-division teams. We had to scrap for our wins—a run here, a run there, a key play in the field, a clutch inning from one of our pitchers.

The Sunday doubleheader against Montreal was no different. We came from behind and won the first game 4–3. The second game was like the first. Rusty Staub homered off Nolan Ryan in the first inning to give the Expos a 2–0 lead. Agee led off with a homer to get one back, and Al Weis doubled in a run in the second to tie the score, but Staub singled home Montreal's third run in the third, and we were behind again, 3–2.

With two out in our third, I got a hit off Howie Reed, Montreal's starter. Shamsky was up behind me, and it was a perfect time to steal second base. I could score from second on a hit. I got a pretty fair jump on Reed and broke for second. They were expecting me to try it, and Johnny Bateman, their catcher, got his throw to second in a hurry. But I felt my foot hit the bag, and then I felt Bobby Wine's tag, and I knew I'd made it. Then I heard the second-base umpire, Frank Dezelan, call me out. I was upset. Not enraged, but upset. Dezelan had called me out on a couple of other plays early in the season that I thought should have gone the other way. I had to let him know that I knew I was safe.

I got up slowly, complaining about the call. I knew it wouldn't be changed, but I figured Dezelan knew he'd blown it. An umpire has to make a split-second decision, then stick by it.

You know they're going to miss some, and so do they. But at least if the man is big enough to admit to himself that he blew one, then maybe he'll give you the benefit of the doubt the next time around. So I told Dezelan I was safe, and then, because I'd made the third out, I began trotting back toward the Met dugout so I could get my glove. That's when Dezelan yelled after me, "What are you complaining about, Jones? It wasn't even close." It took a second for that to register. "It wasn't even *close*." You can understand the man missing a play. He's human. He can say, "Sorry, I missed one," and you walk away without another word. It's a judgment call, and once he's missed it, he's missed it. Even if he'd said nothing, I wouldn't have been bothered. I watch my temper usually, and I rarely curse. I don't really recall exactly what I called him, but it was mean, nasty, dirty, rough, and tough. Before that Sunday I'd only been thrown out of one game in my career, in 1967, when I argued about a third strike at home plate. But Dezelan had to run me out of the game right there. I ran off the field and down the ramp that leads from our dugout into the clubhouse. I was angry with myself for saying things that would get me thrown out of a close game. That could only hurt the team. But I felt that if the Mets were going to be in this pennant race, some of us had better start shouting for our rights pretty soon, before the umpires made enough big decisions against us to take the pennant away.

The Mets were used to getting the short end of it from umpires. In the old days Casey Stengel used to say, "They cheat you because you're terrible." The idea was that we were the Mets, the lovable clowns, the bumblers, who were supposed to do things wrong, expected to foul up. So at times, when we did things right, the umpires would still go against us. And in 1968 and 1969, when we started doing things well often, the umps seemed to be the last men convinced that we were for real. I could understand when they would make calls against us before, because we were a bad team. But when we started to win, to prove we had a good club, the calls still seemed to be going the other way.

Most of the umpires gave us a fair shake, but there were a

Don Jacobsen

"Maybe my daughter doesn't need all the things I needed when I was young, but she does need love."

Angela, Cleon, and Anja.

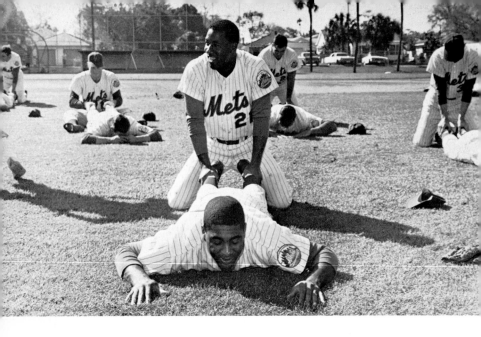

"We felt good about going into the season because we knew we were the most talented Met team ever fielded."

Spring training is a six-week refresher course for the body and mind. Above, Cleon and Tommie Agee pair off for calisthenics. Below, left, Cleon and Bud Harrelson, two of the fleetest Mets, get set for a wind sprint. Below, right, Cleon takes his batting-cage cuts.

Don Jacobsen

"I'd tire of the same girl very quickly—until I met Angela."

The Joneses look over a tray of hamhocks.

"I wanted to return to the people who knew me and helped me when I had nothing."

Cleon at a post-Series reception in Mobile.

Ed Hershey

Wide World

"I touched the plate exactly at 8:43 on the evening of September 10. We were in first place."

Cleon scores on Ken Boswell's single to beat the Expos, 3–2, and the Mets take the lead.

"All that base running had the Braves thinking. And sometimes a man thinks too much."

Cepeda's throw bounces past Didier, and Cleon scores winning run of first play-off game against the Braves.

Wide World

United Press International

"From the first pitch, we were grooving on Jarvis."

Cleon lines a double in Mets' 7–4 victory in the third play-off game against Atlanta.

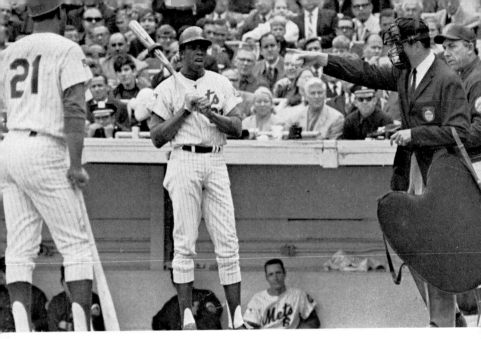

Wide World

"I walked out with Clendenon and told him, 'Look how much I got done with my foot last time. Think what I'd do if I ever used my bat.'"

This sequence marked the turning point of the fifth and final game of the Series. Above, umpire Lou DiMuro awards Cleon first base after examining shoe polish on ball that struck his foot. Moments later, below, Cleon greets Donn Clendenon who followed with a home run.

Stan Wolfson

Stan Wolfson

"The fans had waited an hour and a half just to pat us on the back."

Supposedly sophisticated New York went wild when the Mets won the Series. Above, at Shea Stadium the fans tore away anything they could take for souvenirs. Below, in Times Square and all over the city, ticker tape flew from the skyscrapers.

Don Jacobsen

Bill Senft

"*Sometimes I do get tired of signing autographs, but I never get tired of talking to the kids. I know how I felt when I was young, what I'd have given to be close to a major-league baseball player for just five minutes.*"

Cleon in the clubhouse: there's always one more autograph to sign, one more letter to answer.

few guys who didn't. If an umpire does his job to the best of
his ability, that's all you can ask. Like players and managers,
some umpires are better than others. But if a man screws around
with the game and nonchalants it, tries to act as if he isn't interested, that's another thing. If the umpire acts only to make
things easier on himself, then he's not doing an honest job.

I'll give you an example of where that sort of thing comes
into play. Most of my contact (or any player's contact) with an
umpire comes when I'm at bat. In 1969, as I developed more
confidence as a hitter and the pitchers gained more respect for
me, I saw more bad pitches than I ever had before. I needed a
careful job by the man behind the catcher, because the pitchers
were going to be cutting the corners of the plate on me almost
every time. And when certain umpires were working behind
home plate, calling balls and strikes, I knew I'd be in for a
rough game.

I'm not going to publish any names. I mentioned Dezelan
because the thing with him is a public matter. But a few umpires would favor the pitchers almost openly. If a man came
close to the plate, for them that was a strike. These men didn't
want the outcome to depend on balls and strikes. They wanted
me to be swinging so their job would be easier. To do that they
make a hitter's job impossible.

I thought a lot about umpires, sitting by myself in the clubhouse after being kicked out of the Montreal game. There's a
TV set in the clubhouse, and naturally, whenever a game is
being televised, the set's turned to it. I heard a commotion over
the set, and I grabbed a beer from the cooler and walked over
to see what was happening. I couldn't believe it. The fans,
thousands of them, were waving handkerchiefs at Dezelan and
shouting, "We want Cleon.... We want Cleon.... We want
Cleon."

The first thing that came to my mind was, "See, they saw it.
They know I was safe." Then I realized that not one fan in the
park was close enough to second base to know whether I was
safe or out. All they were saying was that they were behind us.
And I'd never heard or seen anything like it. They kept shouting and waving for a few minutes. A thing like that has to spur

a team on. Our fans were tremendous all season. You wanted to win for yourself, of course, but they made you want to win for them, too.

While the fans were shouting, "We want Cleon," in the fourth inning, Montreal was scoring three more runs to take a 6–2 lead. But we kept scrapping and finally went ahead, 7–6, on a homer by Agee. The Expos came back to tie it, but we got in front for good in the seventh when Agee singled and Swoboda, the man who'd replaced me, knocked him in with another hit. We wound up winning 9–7.

I was dressed by the time the game ended, but I waited in the clubhouse for the team. I was thrown out, and Swoboda knocked in the winning run. It was like that every day. When one man wasn't there, another was. We were beautiful.

We went back to Chicago hoping for a three-game sweep but willing to take two out of three from the Cubs in their park.

We lost the first game on Monday 1–0 despite a five-hitter from Seaver. Tom wasn't as fine as he was at Shea the week before, but he was certainly good enough to win. We just didn't hit for him. Billy Hands gave us six hits, never more than one an inning, and the Cubs put two singles together for a run in the sixth inning.

The next day we won 5–4 because with two out and two on in the fourth inning, Gil stayed with Al Weis, and Weis put one of Dick Selma's pitches on the roof in left field. It was only the fifth homer of Al's career, and it couldn't have come at a better time. We seemed to be doing everything at the right time. The Cubs said we were lucky. But I know it wasn't luck. It was work. I'd seen Hodges and Weis spend time on Al's hitting. A guy like Al—good field, no hit, thirty-one years old—most managers would accept him for what he was and never give him a second look. They'd say something like "Everybody knows he can't hit" and forget it. That gets them off the hook. But Hodges needed a twenty-five-man effort from us, and he knew it. So he worked on twenty-five men. He told Weis things about his swing that he hadn't heard in ten years of organized ball. Then he used him in the games, giving him confidence. The day Weis hit the homer he was still starting at shortstop even though Bud Harrelson was back from Army camp and sitting on the bench. If Gil had pulled Weis the second Bud got back, all the confidence-building would've been destroyed. Instead, Gil took a shot. And Al Weis hit a shot over the roof for him.

The next day we got fourteen hits and won 9–5. Jenkins never knew what hit him. Agee led off the game with a double, Boswell singled him home, I singled and stole second, Garrett walked, Kranepool singled Boswell home, and Martin singled me and Garrett home. That was the first. In the second Jenkins got to throw one pitch. Agee hit a homer. That was the kind of day we had. We were only three and a half games behind. We dressed and walked out into the hot Chicago afternoon to the bus that would take us to the airport for the plane to Montreal. Kids were all around the bus, some of them screaming that we were just lucky, that we'd lose all the rest of our games. The Bleacher Bums, I thought. That's what some fans in the bleachers at Wrigley Field called themselves. As we pulled away from the curb, I remember looking back over my shoulder at them. "We'll be back," I said quietly. "We'll be back in October."

We had Thursday off to relax and enjoy the summer sights of Montreal. During the first game we played there, Friday, two familiar events took place. We won 5–2, and I was thrown out of the game by an umpire.

The Expos had jumped in front of us, but we tied the game for Koosman in the fifth inning, and we still had the bases loaded with two out. I was on second base. Garrett hit a hard liner to right, a hit, and Boswell scored the go-ahead run. With two out, I was running all the way. But Rusty Staub, the Montreal right-fielder, has one of the good arms in baseball, and Garrett's single was hit too hard. Staub's throw was in Ron Brand's catcher's mitt by the time I started my slide into home plate.

Brand, like most catchers in that position, was trying to block the plate, crouching low in the base line so that the runner cannot possibly score before the catcher gets a chance to tag him out. The runner in that position really has no choice. He can't try to slide around the catcher's ankles, because the catcher can simply drop a shin guard on the runner's leg. I've seen a man break his ankle on that play. No, the only choice a runner has, the only choice I had going into Brand, is to hit him hard and hope the catcher drops the ball. If a catcher's going to block the plate, I've got to protect myself physically and give us our best shot at scoring a run.

I went in ready for contact, trying to hit him up around the shin guards with my shins. I could have slid in with my spikes up, but nobody wants to cut a man up. They give you spikes on your shoes for traction, not as a weapon. So I tucked my feet in, as I always do on that play, and went hard with my shins making the contact. He held the ball, although we both went flying after the impact. Apparently Brand thought I'd come in too hard. He got up before I did and started stepping over me to go to the Expo dugout. Then he kicked me.

It was that simple. He kicked me. Some newspapers incorrectly reported that Brand accidentally brushed my arm with his leg. If he did, then you can just as easily say that I accidentally jumped up and brushed his jawbone with my fist. Sure I popped him. I didn't care where I was or who he was, I wasn't about to let anyone kick me. I hit him a couple of quick blows, and then they broke it up. I didn't feel I'd done anything wrong. I'd made the play the way they tell you to make it—hard and clean. And Brand had come back with a clean shot. He should have been satisfied that he'd held the ball and tagged me out. That's the way a catcher's supposed to respond. He blocks the plate, daring me to hit him hard. I hit him hard, and he holds the ball. No complaints. So I felt justified in taking a shot at Brand after he kicked me. And I couldn't believe it when the umpire, Bill Williams, threw me out of the game and let Brand stay in.

"How come I'm out and he isn't?" I asked Williams.

"You threw a punch," he said.

I said, "You could see plain as day that he kicked me. Throw him out, too."

"Kicking," Williams told me, "doesn't count. The guy who throws the first punch is automatically out of the game." I filed that piece of information away for future battles.

Jerry Grote hit a two-run homer in the eighth to give us some breathing room, and Koosman finished strong, so everyone was in good spirits in the clubhouse. All I heard was, "Hey, Jones, what are you going to do next time to get out of playing the whole game?" And everybody laughed. We didn't know then that the next time was less than two weeks away and that it would have nothing to do with an umpire.

We wound up splitting four games with the Expos, and in one of the games over the weekend I pulled my hamstring muscle. That's the muscle behind the knee, and it's an important one for a ballplayer because it functions every time you take a step, every time you bend your knee at the plate. I've always tried to forget about injuries when I could. I didn't tell anyone about the hamstring pull, but Gil noticed it right away. "You're not running as well as you can," he told me. I told him about the pull then, and he told me to make sure I got treatment for it.

Treatment. That means getting to the park early and spending an hour or two on the trainer's table or in the whirlpool bath. I try to avoid treatment. I'm not the type of guy who likes to spend half his life on the trainer's table. Some players are exactly the opposite. They want treatment for this, that, and the other thing. If nothing's really wrong with them, they'll invent something. An hour on the trainer's table is just part of their normal playing day. It's psychological. You go in there and lie down often enough, and pretty soon you feel you have to do it. I don't want that. I'd hurt the hamstring early in 1964 at Buffalo and received treatment all season without helping it much. After the season it came around in a couple of weeks. I decided then that it needed rest, that alcohol rubs and whirlpool baths didn't mean much if you had to go out and run every day after you got them.

But by then I had a new reason for wanting to stay in the lineup and shake off any injury. The All-Star Game was coming up in Washington that Tuesday, and I was the National League's starting left fielder. The All-Star Game is about the only time, during the season, when you think purely as an individual. The rest of the time you have to think for the whole team. When the team wins, you're good; when it loses, you're not. I'm not just saying that; I mean it.

You never stop during the season to say, "Well the team's not doing that well, but I'm getting my hit every day." Not if you want to be a winner, you don't. Instead, you do your best and expect the same from every other player. Nobody should ever have to say he's going to do this for himself and that for the team. It should all be one. In my case, if I hit well enough, I would have to be helping our ball club.

I was happy, overjoyed, when we won, and it didn't matter whether my hit had won the game or not. If I got enough hits and we won enough games, that would have to happen at times.

But the All-Star Game is one of those times when you take credit as an individual. And since the players vote for the teams themselves, it is the best kind of honor a man can receive. When my average stayed up over .350 through June, I thought about whether I'd make it. But I decided that I wouldn't let it disappoint me if I wasn't elected to the first team. It was a fabulous year for outfielders in our league.

The Cincinnati Reds could have fielded the entire National League outfield by themselves with Pete Rose, Alex Johnson, and Bobby Tolan. And the Pirates had three more—Roberto Clemente, Matty Alou, and Willie Stargell. Then there was Hank Aaron from the Braves and Jimmy Wynn from the Astros and Willie Mays, who wasn't having the kind of year that would get him voted on but would probably be picked by Red Schoendienst, the manager, as a reserve because he was Willie Mays.

A couple of weeks before the game we got word that I'd been voted to the starting outfield with Alou and Aaron. The more I thought about the game, the more I decided that I had three goals: I wanted to play more than the three innings that starters had to be played, I wanted the National League team to win, and I wanted to contribute. In the end, it all happened.

Seaver, Koosman and I took off for Washington from Montreal while the rest of the Mets prepared to enjoy a three-day rest. There was a beautiful dinner in Washington to honor baseball's hundredth anniversary. But a player sees a lot of dinners. He also sees a lot of games. The real treat in the All-

Star Game, at least for a first-timer like me, was the clubhouse before the game.

I looked around the room, at the greatest players in the game, and thought to myself, "I'm a part of this. I've dreamed about it all of my life, and I'm here. With Mays, Aaron, McCovey, and all the others. I'm an All-Star."

I was hitting sixth in the National League lineup, but that didn't seem low when I considered that Johnny Bench, the Reds' great young catcher, was hitting seventh, and that three outfielders named Rose, Clemente, and Mays were on the bench. Most of the conversation in the National League clubhouse was about the pennant races. With the two divisions, by the end of July there were still nine teams with a shot at winning—the Cubs, the Mets, the Cards, and the Pirates in our division and every team in the West except the Padres.

Most of the pennant talk was in the form of kidding. Ernie Banks, who was the second-string All-Star first baseman behind McCovey, is always talking. So I tried to jump him. "We're going to beat you and go all the way," I yelled to Ernie. "This is our year." He just laughed and told me what a great ball club the Cubs had.

In the game itself we just had too much power for the American League. We scored a run in the first inning. In the second I got a single off Mel Stottlemyre, and Bench hit a long home run. We knocked Stottlemyre and Blue Moon Odom out with five more runs in the third, and that was it. I played until the seventh inning and got two hits in four at-bats. So I'd accomplished everything I wanted to in Washington.

We went on to Cincinnati and split four games with the Reds and headed back to New York, still four and a half games behind the Cubs.

My leg was still bothering me, but I was treating it, as Hodges had asked, and I wasn't complaining. It rained in New York on Tuesday, the day we were supposed to play the first of two games with the Astros. It had been raining for several days, as a matter of fact, and this was Houston's last trip into New York, so if the games weren't played, they'd have to be rescheduled for the Astrodome later. You know nobody on the Mets wanted that to happen. A doubleheader was scheduled for Wednesday, July 30, to get in the postponed game.

The outfield was terrible. Shea Stadium was built over a swamp, and there isn't a field that gets any wetter after a heavy rain than Shea. The turf was slow and slippery, and I could feel the extra pressure on my sore leg. I went out to see how bad it was before the games, and I remember telling Agee that I didn't know if I could make it but that I'd try. I got two hits in the first game, but Houston beat us 16–3, scoring eleven runs in the ninth inning to really put it out of reach.

In the third inning of the second game the Astros went on another tear, belting Gentry and Ryan all over the place. They already had about six runs in when Johnny Edwards hit a ball down the line in left field. Edwards isn't a very fast runner, but it was a clean double, even on a dry field. On the gook out there that day, there was no chance for me to catch up to the ball on the fly. An inning before, I'd slipped and fallen down on a ball when I'd tried too hard. And in the first inning I'd hit a simple fly ball to short center that became a double because Jimmy Wynn, Houston's center fielder, couldn't reach the ball. Nobody thought Wynn wasn't trying as hard as he could. But with the field as wet as it was, he looked like he was walking in after my ball. The field was worse than I'd ever seen it.

So I played it safe going after Edwards' shot. I caught up to the ball in the left-field corner and threw it to third base. A run had scored, and I didn't see any live play to make on the bases, so I didn't exactly burn the ball into third. I made an ordinary throw. Without an injury, on a dry field in a close game, I might have dived for the ball, but I'm only saying that because of what happened next. At the time I made the play, it seemed so obviously the thing to do that nothing else crossed my mind.

When Gil Hodges walked out of the dugout, I thought he was going out to remove Ryan. But I saw him walk past third base and out into left field, heading straight toward me. He motioned for me to come in, and when I got close, he said, "What's wrong with you? Does your leg bother you?"

"I've got a slight pull, Gil, but I can make it," I told him. Then it dawned on me that Gil might have something more specific in mind. "It's wet out there, Gil," I told him. "And I can't run good, anyway." He knew that. He'd seen that before anyone else had in Montreal a week before.

He said, "If you're not running good, why don't you just come out of the ball game?" Then he turned around and headed toward the dugout. I knew he had something more than my leg in mind, and I followed him in. I ran down the ramp to the clubhouse. Only this time nobody in the stands shouted, "We want Cleon." They'd all seen the play, and they'd all seen Gil take me out of the game.

It was just one of those things. Gil knew what he was doing, I guess. We were getting our socks kicked off by the Astros, and Gil wanted to shake us all up. I didn't think then, and I don't think now, that you take a .350 hitter who's been delivering for you all season and make an example of him. In the club-house I was upset and bitter. I dressed quickly, saying to myself over and over, "Why me? Why did it have to happen to me?"

Hodges had shown me up in front of two major-league base-ball teams, 30,000 fans in the stands, and millions watching on television. He wanted to help the team. I understand that. But so did I. And up until then Gil Hodges had never shown me anything but class. That day he showed me something less. I was upset, but at the same time, right there in the clubhouse, I made up my mind that I wasn't going to let it get me down.

We had too much going for us for me to get down. I knew that I hadn't been loafing, and nobody could tell me that I had been. Hodges had hurt one man to get twenty-four others to come alive, and maybe it wasn't a wrong move if it worked. The more I think about it, the more I believe he didn't plan it. He did it on the spur of the moment because he felt he had to do something to shake us up. I don't know if for one moment Gil really thought I had let myself, him, or the team down on the ball Edwards hit or any other play. Maybe I'll never know. We didn't discuss it that day or the next or any time after that. We probably never will. It's over.

So the stories were printed, and I came out looking like a goat. The first thing I thought about was, "This reminds me of the way it was with Westrum." But I'd already decided that it

wasn't worth getting upset about. We had too much at stake.
It was hard at the time, but I made another promise to myself.
I told myself that I wasn't going to get down on Gil, either,
because that kind of attitude could only hurt me and the team.
The silliest thing a player ever said is, "I'm not going to put out
for *him.*" Who's he hurting? There's no way a player is going
to like everything the manager says or does. Gil Hodges is the
best manager I've ever played for, the most knowledgeable
about his players and the game.

The next day we had another postponed game to make up
with the Astros, and we lost again, 2–0, when Tom Griffin beat
Seaver. Griffin had beaten us 7–0 in Houston earlier in the
season. If he pitched against everyone the way he does against
the Mets, he'd be one of the best in baseball. But of course if
Houston beat everyone the way they beat us, the World Series
would have been played on that synthetic grass at the Astrodome in 1969 instead of on our beautiful swamp in Flushing.

I didn't play in the Thursday game against the Astros or on
Friday night when we beat the Atlanta Braves. On Saturday
night Gil asked me if I felt I could pinch-hit. It was the first
thing he'd said to me since Wednesday. I said yes.

Jim McAndrew was pitching for us that night against Ron
Reed, a tall right-hander who was good enough to play forward
in the National Basketball Association. We'd never beaten
Reed. He was 2–0 against us in 1968, 2–0 in 1969. In the bottom
of the seventh the score was still 0–0. Swoboda walked, and we
got him into scoring position, and McAndrew was due to hit.
There were left-handed hitters on the bench—Shamsky, Martin,
Boswell. But we needed a hit, and I was hitting .350. Gil told
me to get a bat and go up to hit.

I wasn't thinking about redeeming myself or proving myself
or any of that dramatic nonsense. You don't win games with
daydreams. I was only thinking about two things: what Reed
would throw and where I could hit it. I got a hit, Swoboda
scored, and we won 1–0. Hodges sent Seaver out to run for me,
and when I came back to the dugout, he shook my hand. There
were no words between us. He'd asked me to do a job, and I'd
done it. That's why both of us had come to the park that night.

On Sunday Gentry fell behind 5–0, and in the fifth I pinch-hit for him and got a two-run single off Milt Pappas. We scored five to tie, and Grote won it for us in the eleventh inning with a homer. But now it was August, and a win could make us only half happy. The Cubs had to start losing, and they weren't doing it yet. They'd won both their games against Cincinnati Saturday and Sunday to stay six ahead.

The next night we lost to Jim Maloney in Cincinnati 1–0 to fall seven games back. We lost three out of four to the Reds, took three out of four in Atlanta, then went to Houston. The first night Tom Griffin beat us 3–0. Then we lost the next two there. We flew back to New York in third place, nine and a half games behind the Cubs and a game behind the Cardinals. Another game or two and we could fall to fourth place, because the Pirates were right behind us.

In New York there were stories in the papers about how the Cards had nine games left with the Cubs and were finally ready to make their run. The stories didn't even mention the Mets.

We were supposed to open up a home stand against the Padres the next night, but it rained. In the old days one of the bad jokes about the Mets was that we counted rainouts as wins. This rain had forced us into two doubleheaders in the next two days, since this was San Diego's last trip in. But it was worth it. We'd played seventeen games in fifteen days, eleven of them on the road, and the rain meant two days off in a row. It gave us a chance to rest, a chance to think.

11

Catching the Cubs

We won twelve out of our next thirteen games, just the streak we needed to fight back into the race.

And just as in our two previous big winning streaks, we were winning games in surprising ways with startling players. Every day we had a different hero. There was hardly a man on the team who wasn't playing the best ball of his life, who didn't deliver when it came down to winning or losing. And there were a lot of those moments, because we weren't exactly destroying the league. We were getting a run here, a run there, just enough to win. But that's all you need.

Saturday, August 16, Tom Seaver beat the Padres 2–0 in the first game, and Jim McAndrew beat them 2–1 in the second. The next day, we won two games by 3–2 scores, on a three-run homer by Duffy Dyer in the first game and a two-run triple by Bud Harrelson in the second. Four wins in two days. We were back in second place with a 66–51 record, seven and a half games behind the Cubs.

The Giants, who were in the middle of the pennant fight in the other division, came in August 19 with Marichal ready to start a three-game series against Gentry. If you're the Giants, this is one game you count on winning. You've got your stopper out there against a rookie. And that night Marichal was about as strong as he can be. Only Gentry was just as good, if not better. The only thing Juan might have had on Gary was stamina. In the tenth inning Gary was tired. Juan looked like he could shut us out for another ten. Hodges had McGraw ready for the eleventh as we went to bat in the bottom of the tenth with the score still 0–0.

One way you try to get an edge on Marichal is by running the bases. He's got a big motion that makes stealing a little easier. In the tenth I got a hit, was sacrificed to second, and stole third. But I died there, just as I'd died at second back in the fourth after another single and a stolen base. Aside from my two singles, we'd gotten only one hit in the ten innings.

We didn't get anything going in the eleventh, but McGraw was stopping the Giants. In the twelfth I got another hit with one out, and McGraw bunted. Marichal slipped coming off the mound and then threw the ball off Tug's back and into right field. McGraw and Ron Hunt, who was covering first, both went down. I kept running. The third-base coach, Eddie Yost, waved me home. It would take a perfect play to get me. The Giants made a perfect play. Hunt recovered, ran the ball down, and fired a strike to the plate. I was out. I didn't feel too bad. When you take the play to the other team, play aggressively, and they stop you, then you've got no complaints.

Sometimes you can even be aggressive in the field at the right moment. And one of those moments came in the top of the thirteenth, with two out and McCovey coming up. Hodges ordered us to go into a special shift, sending our third baseman, Bobby Pfeil, into left field and swinging the other three out-fielders around toward right.

The idea was that with two out and none on, Willie McCovey could hurt us only with a long ball. And he's so capable of doing it that we were willing to concede him an easy single if he would give up his chance for an extra-base hit. Sure, Mc-Covey could bunt the ball down the third-base line or reach out and swat an easy grounder to the left side for a hit. But it wouldn't be an extra-base hit, and if he defied us and took his normal cut, the four outfielders would make that harder to get.

Those kinds of shifts are used from time to time against power hitters. Ted Williams and Mickey Mantle saw them, and we'd used one before against Richie Allen of the Phillies. If you get a man's concentration off just a little bit, then you've accomplished something with that kind of thing. Even in the field, on defense, you're being aggressive, challenging the man, maybe initiating the play. But it's a funny thing about the real good ones. They don't shake easily. With two out in the thirteenth, Willie McCovey wasn't going for singles.

He hit a drive to deep left field. Because of our four-outfielder shift, I reached the ball sooner than I would have, but reaching the ball wasn't the problem. Keeping the ball in the park was what I had to worry about. I planted a foot at the base of the wall, which is eight feet high. If I could use the wall as a brace for my jump, then I wouldn't crash into it and jar the ball loose on the way down.

I crouched, jumped, caught the ball at the very top of the wall, then leaned forward, sticking my butt out as a cushion against the fence. I landed on the grass and rolled over, with the ball still in my glove. "Hold 'em right there," Agee yelled to me on the way in. "I'll think of something." One thing about that Agee. He's one hell of a thinker. With one out in the fourteenth, Tommie hit the ball out of the place and we won 1–0.

We split our next two against the Giants and beat the Dodgers three straight to finish our home stand five and a half games out of first. Every one of our victories over the Dodgers was a come-from-behind win. We were getting the key hits, and our bullpen was holding up beautifully. Tug McGraw got a save in the first game against L.A., and Ron Taylor and Cal Koonce won the other two. Among them, McGraw, Taylor, and Koonce had a 19–9 record with twenty-eight saves. It was like having at least one extra twenty-game winner on our staff.

We flew to San Diego to start a Western trip with a twi-night doubleheader August 26, and we won twice behind Seaver and McAndrew. I got hurt in the first game. I was on first base, and Shamsky singled to right. It was a sharply hit ball, and I tried to decoy the outfielder into thinking I would stop at second. When he'd committed himself to a soft throw, I broke for third. I made it with a slide, but I slid fairly close to the bag at third, and I was in danger of oversliding the base, so I reached out with my hand to try to stop. I stopped all right, but I also jammed my hand against the base.

It was a slight sprain, but it bothered me a lot at the plate. I played the second game and the next night, when Koosman won to bring us within two games of the Cubs. But it was no use. Every time I swung, it felt as if I was spraining the hand all over again. I needed a rest, even though the last thing I wanted to do was sit down.

I sat in San Francisco and Los Angeles, and we lost four out of seven. Just like that, we were five games out of first again. The Cubs, who'd faded badly in the last two weeks of August, picked up some quick ground in Atlanta and Cincinnati.

My hand was still sore when we returned to New York, and I sat out our four-game series against the Phillies, but we won three of the four, and the Cubs lost three straight to the Pirates in Chicago. Now the Cubs were coming back to Shea for two games, and they were only two and a half games in front of us, only one game in the loss column.

Contenders talk about the loss column a lot in September. With rainouts and scheduling differences, two teams rarely have the same number of games played at any one time before the end of the year. The Cubs were coming in with an 84–56 record to our 80–57. We were two and a half games behind (each win or loss counts a half-game), but we only had one more loss. As the season gets shorter and shorter, you like to think you're capable of winning every game, so you assume your remaining games are going to be won. In our thinking, Chicago had 56 losses and we had 57, so we were really only a game behind the Cubs. And with our last two games scheduled for Wrigley Field the first two days in October, we knew all we had to do was stay within two games of the Cubs to have a chance for the Eastern Division pennant.

Gil held me out of the Phillie games because he didn't want to take a chance on losing me for Chicago. Neither of us knew whether my hand was ready for the first game against the Cubs, September 8, because part of my treatment was not to use the hand at all. But I took batting practice, and the hand felt all right. I could tell my timing was off because of the ten-day layoff, but I decided I had to give it a shot. Every day I was out would put me one day farther away from my hitting groove.

While Hodges had been planning for the Cubs, Durocher had been fighting for his life. Chicago had lost five straight, and Leo was dying. We had Seaver ready for the Wednesday night game, Koosman ready for Tuesday's. Jenkins, the Cubs' best pitcher, had been used over the weekend, and he wasn't going to pitch at all. But after Koosman beat Bill Hands 3–2 on Tuesday, Durocher pulled Holtzman and started Jenkins on Wednesday against Seaver.

It was best against best, but our best was rested (and he just might have been a little better than their best, anyway). In the first inning Agee and I walked, and Boswell doubled us both home. In the third I singled. We were two up, and the Cubs hadn't gotten a hit off Seaver. The Chicago first baseman was Willie Smith. Banks had run out of gas. But he was still talking a good game. "You guys are never going to see first place," he told me before the game. "How can you win with a high school team?"

I laughed. "You're tired, and you're about ready to give it up," I told old Ernie. "You're the guys with the high school team—only you have the coach playing first base." There aren't too many high school teams, I thought to myself, who have a chance to walk home with 20,000 bucks. The money was on everybody's mind. But for the team coming after it from behind, it's an incentive. For the guys who've been holding it all season, trying to take it to the bank, it's a burden. In their minds, they can't win the money. They've already got it, and they can only lose it. And the Cubs dropped another hunk of it in that third inning.

Shamsky forced me at second. Then when Boswell missed a hit-and-run pitch, Art was caught between first and second in a rundown. Art will never be confused with Maury Wills on the bases, but he didn't give up. He forced the Cubs to make the play, and they couldn't. Smith ended up throwing the ball off Beckert's glove, and Shamsky was safe. Boswell struck out. It would've been the third out of the inning if Shamsky hadn't broken the rundown. But he had, and that gave Clendenon three swings at Jenkins. He only needed one for a two-run homer. We scored three more runs off Jenkins and won 7–1 with a five-hitter from Seaver. We were only a half-game behind and actually a game ahead in the loss column.

I had to feel that the Cubs were a dead team. They *were* tired. You could see it on their faces and in their play. Seaver and Koosman, our stoppers, had done their job.

The word "stopper" has popped up often in my descriptions of Tom and Jerry. It ought to be explained. A stopper is a man who's expected to win. He's an excellent pitcher—good arm, smart selection of pitches, excellent control, and, most important, consistency. When you go out to play behind Seaver or Koosman, you know you're going to be in the game for nine innings. It's the kind of feeling the Giants get when Marichal pitches and the Cardinals have when Gibson's going. It affects your play.

A stopper goes out and throws strikes, and it keeps his fielders in the game. You're on your toes on every pitch, and it pays off. It's not a coincidence that a team makes more good plays behind a great pitcher. When I know Seaver's the starting pitcher, I wake up in the morning feeling good, and I go to the park that way. When the game starts, I stand out in left field ready and anxious to have the ball hit at me. I'm watching every move on the field.

On the other hand, if your pitcher throws a strike every now and then and has no command of what he's doing, it becomes a chore to stand 300 feet away and stay in the game. You tend to get back on your heels, and you're not as alert. You're not as ready to go after a ball as you should be, and you find yourself caught out of position. I try to prevent that by playing little games with myself out there. I'll say to myself, "The batter's going to hit the next pitch at me." But you can only fool yourself for so long. The pitcher will throw three or four useless pitches in a row, and before I know it, I'm out of the game, mentally speaking. I'm thinking about what I might do my next time up at the plate or daydreaming about something. But when your man on the mound is throwing strikes, you don't have time to lose your concentration because something's happening on every pitch.

In the long run the best thing a stopper does, of course, is

win games. If you've got a bad team, he can make you respectable. If you've got a good team, he can make you a pennant-
winner. And even though nobody seemed ready to give us
enough credit even in early September, the Mets were a good
team. We had more than Seaver and Koosman. We had good
second-line pitching, a deep bullpen, and solid defense, and by
September we had the hitting we needed.

Agee was the kind of leadoff hitter who'd get a pitcher off
balance because not only was he a threat to hit one into the
seats, he also had the speed of a leadoff man.

Actually, I would have been happier to see Tommie hitting
second because we never did find a consistent number-two man.
We went with Gaspar and Boswell a lot early in the season, and
Gil finally settled on Garrett against righties and Harrelson
against lefties. Rusty and Bud each made a lot of key plays—
almost all of us did—but they didn't hit for average, and many
times our second hitter would make the third out with me on
deck. Not only would that leave men on base, it would put me
up first in the following inning. A batter is always at a disad-
vantage when he leads off an inning because the pitcher has
more of a chance to work on him. With men on base, you
usually see better pitches to hit.

I usually hit third. Behind me we had Shamsky and Kranepool against righties, Swoboda and Clendenon against lefties.
Grote did most of the catching. When Gil felt he needed another left-handed bat against a particularly tough right-handed
pitcher, he went to J. C. Martin. Part of his plan for giving
Weis more confidence in his hitting ability was making Al a
one-way hitter. Two times nothing is nothing. So Gil made Weis
hit only right-handed, and that worked fine, too, because he
could play against left-handers, with Boswell, the second baseman, against righties.

You look at the averages and you wonder how that lineup
could have won a pennant, but if you saw the games in August
and September, you wonder why everyone on the team didn't
hit .300. We won the big games, the close games, the extra-
inning games. And time and time again we won with the unexpected. You never knew who would make the big fielding

play or come up with the key hit. But somebody always seemed to.

It may have been as close to a complete twenty-five-man team effort as you can find in the history of baseball.

As this style began to win for us, it had a definite effect on the way we behaved on and off the field. You hear stories about different cliques on a lot of teams. The veterans hang together; the Southerners hang together; the blacks hang together. We had no cliques on the Mets. And we didn't have two players who didn't get along with each other.

On the road Tommie and I roomed together. But we hung around with Boswell and Shamsky, going to dinner or to the movies. And at home Angela and I went to parties at the Kranepools' and the Grotes'. At the time I never thought about the fact that some of us were black and some of us were white. Maybe I'm being naïve, but I don't think anyone else did, either.

Except when it comes to signing contracts, I don't consider myself a mathematical whiz. But somebody once figured out that with twenty-five players, four coaches, and the manager you have 575 separate relationships on a baseball team. Multiply that by 162 games, and you can understand how easy it is for a clubhouse to be coming apart at the seams by the middle of the summer. But ours just got closer and closer together.

Everybody was warm and likable. Nobody wisecracked about someone else unless he was sure it was something that wouldn't hurt the man. You have to kid around to stay loose, but I've seen men come to blows over a wisecrack. Yet nothing like that ever happened to us in 1969. And except for one time, nobody popped off, either.

That exception was the day Hodges pulled me off the field and we lost those two horrible games to Houston. Swoboda yelled and said guys were letting down. Ron's an emotional guy. We all felt bad when things didn't go well. We all wanted to win. But he's the kind of cat who has to let it out. The next day he came around and apologized all over the clubhouse. "I'm sorry," he said. "I didn't mean anything by it. You know me, I just say what comes into my head."

But that was the only time we ever had anything like that, and it was really nothing at all. I can't help comparing this atmosphere to the Cub clubhouse the July day Don Young played the balls Boswell and I hit into doubles at Shea Stadium. First Durocher tore Young apart, and then Ron Santo and some of the other regulars sounded off on him. How was the team going to benefit? The kid wouldn't. He was already shaken. He hadn't *tried* to make those mistakes. He wanted to catch those balls. I've seen Curt Flood and Willie Mays and just about every great outfielder in the National League have bad days against that bad Shea background. Young made a mistake or two. It cost Chicago a game. But so what? When Santo makes an error, he says to himself, "Well, hell, I'm only human."

I wonder, if Santo had stopped and put himself in Young's place, whether he'd have popped off like that. Besides, if Young really was letting down out there, what did it say about the Cubs? Sure, they had a problem in center field. It didn't take a baseball expert to figure that out. But how were Santo and Durocher going to solve it by knocking this kid?

I don't mean to rap the Cubs. Things like that happen in a lot of clubhouses. You read about them every season, and you'd better believe that for every incident you read about there are ten that you don't. But in 1969 nothing like that happened in the Met clubhouse.

As long as I've touched on the subject, let's discuss what the fans read about baseball teams. The baseball writers like to think they know everything that's going on. Of course they don't. But they do try to find things out. They'll pick up a little bit of this conversation, a few words of that one, and add it up. Once in a while they get a good story. Sometimes they blow things out of proportion when they go rumor-hunting like that.

But most of the writers' stories aren't about rumors; they're about games. And whether we win or lose, the writers need a story. I understand that. If we lose a tough one, Angela knows she ought to go easy on the conversation. If it weren't for Anja after some of those games, the house would be awful quiet. (Anja holds the Shea Stadium record for falling asleep during the most crucial games in one season and the Jones apartment record for making life livable after almost every loss.) But even after a tough loss the writers are there, asking questions. They have to have their quotes, whether they're about the homer that's won a game or the strikeout that's lost it.

A player has to accept the writers and be prepared for them. It isn't so much planning what to say after a game as it is planning what not to say. I try not to let them get me over a barrel, in a position where I'll say something I'm going to be sorry to see in print. The writers have seen the game. They know what happened. It's the "why" that they're interested in. That's fine. But at times they try to tell you the "why" and get you to agree with them. They try to pull something out of you that wasn't there in the first place.

A couple of maybes and a nod of your head, and the next day you're in the headlines. It's something you have to be aware of when they're standing in front of your locker after a game. Then you also have to know something about the guy who's interviewing you. Some of the writers are second-guessers. Others are psychologists. They talk to you for ten minutes and psychoanalyze you for a million people the next day. You have to laugh those guys off. One of them wrote that my career turned around because I got my teeth fixed. When I was a kid, I ate some things that weren't good for my teeth, and I didn't get the dental care my daughter's getting today. I wound up with a mouthful of bad teeth. When I could afford it, I had them fixed. But my new teeth have never hit a curve ball or caught a line drive.

Then there was all the stuff about my scar. The psychological writers loved my scar. Here's what one guy wrote in July:

> The scar is a reverse J-shape. It runs down Cleon Jones' right cheek, then turns toward his lip and under his nose, rising again toward his nostril. It is almost like a line on a graph and you can chart Jones' progress by it.
>
> There was a time the Mets' leftfielder was reluctant to discuss the disfigurement of his face, just as he wouldn't talk about himself or his chances of becoming what he has become for the Mets.

"For so long," says Cleon, "I felt as if I was an outsider. I was so uncertain about so many things. I kept asking myself, 'Do I belong here?'"

Go down to Plateau and ask anyone if my scar changed me one bit. I got married after the accident, I signed a baseball contract, and I did everything I would have done before. If I were a movie actor instead of an outfielder, maybe the scar would have bothered me. But it didn't. Sure I didn't say much, for just the reasons I told the writer. I didn't know if I belonged, if I was good enough to play in the major leagues. Where I come from, the way I was raised, you do first and talk second. I was always quiet among strangers. Reluctant to talk about the scar? I really don't remember anybody running up and saying, "Hey, baby, that's a neat scar you have on your face. How'd you get it?" And I wasn't going to walk into the clubhouse and announce to the world how and why my face had been cut up. But in 1969 the Mets were contenders, and there were writers who wanted to tell the world that we were winning because of my auto accident or Seaver's political beliefs or Koosman's ability to milk cows. You don't make a big deal of denying that kind of baloney. You just laugh it off to your friends and hope nobody out there really takes it too seriously.

Television is a little different. You have to be extra careful of what you're saying, because *everything* goes out over the air. But once you've developed some poise and learned to relax in front of a camera, you learn to like it. At least on TV you're speaking for yourself.

12

Only Winners Laugh at Bad Jokes

After our two-game sweep of Chicago the Cubs went to Philadelphia and we stayed in New York for a twi-night doubleheader against the Expos. We were tied 2–2 in the twelfth inning when I singled, and with two out, Gaspar, who'd replaced Shamsky for defense, walked. That brought Boswell up. Bozzy had started playing second base regularly when I hurt my hand—we needed more hitting with me out—and he was in the groove. He hit a solid single, and I scored easily. I touched the plate exactly at 8:43 on the evening of September 10. We were in first place.

We got six runs in the third inning of the second game, and Nolan Ryan breezed home on a three-hitter 7–1. Long before he got the last three outs in the ninth inning, the scoreboard told us that the Phillies had handed the Cubs their seventh straight loss, 4–3. We were loud and funny in the clubhouse, but there was something very serious I thought ought to be said. When the writers came around, I said it.

"Look," I told them. "When we lost, everyone made jokes. Now we're winners. This is real, not fantasy, whether the world wants to accept it or not. Look at the plays we've made to stay in games, throws we've made to save games, hits we've made to win games. We've done everything a pennant contender should do—and we've done it day in and day out. What else do we have to do?"

The writers looked at me as if I were spoiling their fun. But

I had to say it. We were winners, not because we had a double whammy on the other teams or we had an incredible amount of good luck or because anyone had given us any gifts. But I could hear on radio and TV and read in the newspapers and magazines that it would take even more to convince the world that we were for real.

In the meantime we had to convince the Cubs and the rest of the National League. And unfortunately, we had to do it without me. The next day Gary Gentry shut the Expos out 4–0, and the Cubs lost again. But there was a pop fly to short left that I dove for during the game. I felt something give immediately. I thought I'd strained my back on the play. The next night we had a twi-night doubleheader in Pittsburgh. I went out before the first game to take batting practice, and after one swing I turned around to see who'd run into the cage and stabbed me in the side. That's what it felt like. We took X rays and discovered that I had torn a rib. Rest, the doctor said. We were clinching a pennant and he told me to rest.

So for the next ten days I rested. Once or twice I tried to loosen up, but I knew it just wasn't there. I wanted to get back very badly. I was leading the league in hitting, with a .346 average, and I'd really found the groove after my return from the hand injury. I felt I could hit .355. But I also knew it was more important that I be ready for the play-offs and, hopefully, the World Series. So for the next ten days I became a fan. And I thought players had it hard.

As difficult as the bench was for me, it was better than it had been in years past. I'd been on the bench then not because of injury but because someone thought I couldn't get the job done. And before the 1969 season the players who weren't in the game would hang out in the runway or mope around. Now the dugout was alive.

Most teams have bench jockeys, usually coaches or utility players who are very good at getting at opponents. But our best bench jockey was Seaver. On the days he didn't pitch, Tom did two things. He studied the other team's hitters, and he razzed the hell out of the other team's pitcher. You wouldn't believe some of the things that clean-cut All-American boy said when there was about $20,000 a man on the line.

I did some yelling, too, and I also tried to help some of our hitters. Two guys I studied in particular were Agee and Boswell, because both are such streak hitters: one week murder, the next week nothing. Usually it's not an accident; it's a case of bad habits.

Tommie has a tendency to commit himself on a pitch before he ought to. The clue for me is whether he drops his hands before going into his swing. Boswell's got a different problem. He has a short, compact swing. He has to lunge at the ball when he decides to swing or else he loses his effectiveness. In September I noticed that Bozzy was striding into the ball and his bat was coming around too slowly. I got him lunging again, and he started making better contact.

We won two games in Pittsburgh to go three and a half games up on the Cubs. Jerry Koosman won the first game 1–0 on a hit by Jerry Koosman. Don Cardwell won the second game 1–0 on a hit by Don Cardwell.

We split the next two games in Pittsburgh and won one in St. Louis, even though Steve Carlton struck out nineteen batters. Think about that one for a minute. In seventy years of major-league baseball, both leagues, no pitcher had ever struck out nineteen men in a game. Carlton did—and we still beat him, on two two-run homers by Swoboda.

In Montreal we had Koosman and Seaver again. The final scores were 5–0 and 2–0. We were five games ahead of the Cubs with thirteen to play.

We headed back to Shea Stadium for a five-game series against the Pirates, and we got a very scary reminder that good things don't come easy. We lost a twi-night doubleheader Friday night, and on Saturday Bob Moose pitched a no-hitter against us. The guys walked into the clubhouse after Saturday's game telling each other we shouldn't panic. That's the first sign of a team about to panic. But we got some reassurance soon after we'd lost our game. In Chicago the Cardinals had beaten the Cubs. We were still four games in front.

Our little slump made me doubly unhappy because I was still

tied to the bench. I felt I could help our hitting and win the batting championship, too. Instead, I was useless. It could've been the greatest competitive stretch of my life. But I'd go to the park, put on my uniform and a windbreaker, trot around a little bit, and sit down. I couldn't run hard or throw or swing a bat.

Half my problem was solved the next day. Koosman and Cardwell beat the Pirates, and our lead was back up to four and a half games. But the Cardinals were coming in with Briles, Gibson, and Carlton ready to try to keep us from clinching. Gil called me into his office. "I don't want to put you in unless you're ready," he told me. "If it's a matter of one or two days more, we shouldn't take any chances."

So I stayed out of the first two games with St. Louis. Seaver won the first one 3–1 for his twenty-fourth victory. The next night Gibson got a 2–0 lead on us, but we managed a couple of runs, and we had a 2–2 tie in the eighth when the Cards loaded the bases against McGraw. Gibson was up, and he hit a shot to right center. One run had to score, maybe two, unless Swoboda could short-hop the ball and fire home. But Rocky was going to try to no-hop it. If he missed, it was a triple. He didn't miss. He dove and came up with the ball and saved the game. We won it in the eleventh.

My ribs felt better. I knew they felt better because ten days earlier the doctor had said it would take ten days for them to heal. I'd served my time. Actually, they still hurt like hell, but I couldn't sit around any longer. I wanted to be in on the pennant-clinching, and I wanted to be ready for the play-offs.

Clendenon hit two homers and Charles hit one, and we beat the Cardinals 6–0 on Gentry's shutout to win the Eastern Division pennant. All hell broke loose, of course, after the last out.

We had expected that, and I was prepared for it—I thought. Before the game Agee had said to me, "Hey, you know if we're out there when the last out's made, those fans'll be all over the place. We'll have a helluva time getting back to the dugout. Why don't we ask the guys in the bullpen to leave the gate open after the eighth inning? We can beat the crowd through the gate and get to the clubhouse the back way."

That sounded fine to me. I love the fans at Shea, and I felt this was their victory as much as ours, but I wanted to get with the team as fast as I could. Besides, my hand was still sore from one injury, and my ribs hadn't healed completely from another. A man can get hurt in one of those mob scenes. Since Tommie, in center field, is closer to the bullpen than I am in left, we decided that he'd call over to one of the guys in the bullpen and tell them to open the gate.

Tommie checked and was told that the gate couldn't be left open because of security. But in the excitement of the moment, or so he said later, Agee forgot to tell me the gate would be closed.

With one out in the ninth inning, Gary Gentry got Joe Torre to hit into a double play. We were Eastern champions. "The gate," I remembered. I took off for the bullpen, and immediately, I knew something was fouled up. Out of the corner of my eye I saw Agee running the opposite way, toward the dugout. When I got to the gate, I found out why. It was locked.

I turned around to a scene I'll never forget. The fans hadn't reached the outfield yet, but they were everywhere else. Most of them were kids. They were running around with pieces of sod they'd ripped up or any other souvenir they could find. I grabbed my hat and tucked it and my glove under my arm, carrying them like a football.

I had scored twenty-six touchdowns in my senior year at high school, more than any player in the history of the state of Alabama. But there were only eleven guys allowed to tackle me those days. By the time I got started for my 100-yard run from the bullpen to the dugout, there were thousands out there. And I couldn't run out of bounds.

By the time I reached the clubhouse, most of the champagne was on the carpet. Agee saw me right away. "Hey, Beep," he yelled, "what took you so long?" I'll remember Agee's face for a long time. All that champagne all over everybody, and Agee, with that innocent look, asking, "What took you so long?"

After I'd recovered again, I tried to tell anybody who'd listen that we had earned all this, that we were the best team in the league. That wasn't technically true. Actually, we were only the best team in the Eastern Division. A week later we'd be in Atlanta or San Francisco to begin a best-of-five series for the National League championship. Houston had fallen back in early September, and Los Angeles and Cincinnati had dropped out of the Western race. So it was down to the Braves and the Giants. And frankly, we were all rooting for Atlanta.

We'd beaten both the Giants and the Braves eight out of twelve times during the season, but in a short series the Giants looked tougher. They had better pitching with Marichal, Perry, and McCormick, and they had a man who could break up a game any time he came up to bat, Willie McCovey. The Braves were hot, but they didn't have a sound team. Phil Niekro, their best pitcher, hadn't beaten us all season. And although Ron Reed was murder on us, we had to feel he wasn't really as good as he'd been against us. And after Niekro and Reed, the Braves didn't have much. We'd scored more than five runs a game against their staff compared to less than four runs a game against everyone else.

True, they could hit. Aaron was having one of his best all-round years at bat, Cepeda and Carty were taking turns winning games, and there were four other guys who could hurt you with the stick—Tony Gonzalez, Felix Millan, Felipe Alou, and Clete Boyer. But we had the good pitching, and they weren't going to score that much off us. It's one of the oldest rules of baseball: Good pitching beats good hitting.

While I was resting my torn rib, both Pete Rose and Roberto Clemente fell into the .330's. But then they started to come on. They were only a couple of percentage points away by the time I got back into the lineup. Before the second injury I was as confident and comfortable at the plate as I had been all season. I thought I could hit .355, at least. But when I did get back, ten days of doing nothing had robbed me of my rhythm. And the ribs were still sore.

The day after we clinched the pennant Hodges called me into his office. He asked me how my ribs felt and whether I needed a day or two more to rest. I told him that I wasn't perfect, but I had to get ready for the play-offs. I needed the work.

Then he looked at me, without changing his expression, and said, "Are you thinking about winning the batting title?"

Usually, you don't want to admit to any personal ambitions when your team's in a pennant race. The idea is to win games. But we had already clinched the Eastern title. "Gil, I'd like to win it," I said. "But it really doesn't mean that much to me now, not with a chance to get into the World Series. I just want to be ready for next week."

Gil said he had an idea that could help me both ways. He suggested that I lead off for our last five games instead of hitting third. The way Rose and Clemente were coming on, I'd need as many times at bat (and hits) as I could get. And every extra time up might bring my hitting closer to form. I told Gil that it sounded good.

So I hit first for the last five games of the year, three shutout victories in Philadelphia and a split of our two October games in Chicago. And I didn't hit worth a damn because it all felt so strange to me. It was almost like starting the season all over again. I went five for twenty-four in the last six games and lost six points to .340. Rose hit .450 the final week and won it with a .348 to .345 for Clemente. But I got a couple of hits in the last game at Chicago, and I felt I'd done my job. I was a lot more ready for the Braves.

The Braves had come on strong and won the Western Division title. We were going to Atlanta to play the first two games of the play-offs Saturday, October 4, and Sunday, October 5. Then we'd come back to Shea for as many of the last three games as we'd need. The winner would go on to play in the World Series against the American League pennant winner, either Baltimore or Minnesota. If you won it all, you could pick up as much as $20,000 a man in extra money. At least half our team wasn't making $20,000 for the whole season, and all we had to do was win seven games to get an extra $20,000.

We respected Atlanta, but we knew we were better. The one man we felt we had to stop was Hank Aaron. He could be an equalizer. And we didn't stop Aaron at all. But in the end we didn't have to, because they didn't have a pitcher in the park who could get us out. All season long even those people who admitted we were legitimate contenders said we'd make it only on pitching, pitching and luck. After the Atlanta series they couldn't say that anymore.

The opening game was Seaver against Niekro, strength against strength. And we knew Tom was stronger. Niekro was a knuckle-ball pitcher, primarily. When he had to show you his other stuff, he could be tagged. We did a good job of tagging him, two runs in the second inning, two more in the fourth. But Seaver wasn't himself. He'd had an extra couple of days' rest because we clinched the pennant with a week to spare, and maybe his pitching rhythm had been affected. Tom said he didn't feel comfortable out on the mound, and I know he didn't look it. He was rushing his pitches, and even from left field I could tell his control was off.

In the bottom of the seventh Aaron hit a line drive homer over my head in left, and we were down 5–4, six outs away from losing the first play-off game. But we'd been behind before.

Garrett led off the eighth with a double inside the third-base line. Niekro had held me hitless until then, and I wasn't looking to be a hero. I just wanted to meet the ball. A knuckler is a crazy pitch. It's released from the fingertips without any spin. Now, every ball has to spin if you throw it in the air. So somewhere between the mound and the plate a knuckler picks up a spin, and it starts going in the direction of the spin. It can take off or drop or head in one direction or the other. Anyone can *throw* a knuckler. Ballplayers do it all the time on the sidelines, just for fun. The skill is to *control* a knuckler, to get enough of them over the plate so you don't have to throw anything else for strikes. With the tying run on second and none out, I didn't want to give Niekro a couple of free strikes. I was swinging at anything in the strike zone. I didn't exactly tear the cover off the ball. I hit a looper to left and a hit all the way, and Garrett scored the tying run.

Shamsky singled me to second, and Gil gave Boswell the bunt sign. But it's tough to bunt a knuckler. Kenny missed, and I was dead. I'd been so anxious to avoid a force play at third that I'd cheated a couple of steps before the ball reached the plate. Now Chuck Didier, the Braves' rookie catcher, had me caught off base. All he had to do was run right at me, force me to go one way or the other, and throw to whichever base I ran at. It's a book play, the kind of thing a coach will go over with his catchers on the first day of spring training. But sometimes in the middle of a game a rookie will get a little excited.

The only chance I had was to decoy Didier into committing himself too soon. I was so far off second that even if he waited and made sure I was heading there, pumped his arm once, he'd still have me. But as soon as I started heading back, he fired. That was what I'd counted on. I was never going to second; I took a half step back, then went ahead, full speed ahead. I beat the throw—from home to second to third—and our rally was still going.

I had one more good act left in me on the bases. When Boswell bounced back to Niekro, I made a flash move toward the plate, then dove back into third. Niekro had to see whether I was really going or not, and by the time he got the ball to second for the force on Shamsky, Boswell had reached first. Then Kranepool hit a grounder to first, and this time I had to make a move to keep us out of a double play. Cepeda would have had me by ten feet at the plate, so I stopped. I was looking for a rundown. Then maybe I could stay alive at least until Boswell and Kranepool had reached second and third.

All that base running had the Braves thinking. And sometimes a man thinks too much. Cepeda started to go home with the ball, and in the middle of his motion he had second thoughts about the play. But it was too late. What developed was a compromise. He threw it halfway home, and the ball bounced past Didier. I trotted across the plate to give us a 6–5 lead. Niekro walked Harrelson to load the bases and get to Seaver. But Gil figured Seaver had thrown enough pitches by then anyway. He sent J. C. Martin up, and Martin lined a single to center. When Tony Gonzalez let the ball skip by him out there, all three runners scored, and we led 9–5. Ron Taylor got the last six Atlanta outs. We laughed our way into the clubhouse. We'd gotten away with a mediocre game from Seaver and still won. Now we had Koosman going for us, and we weren't going to get two mediocre games in a row—not from Seaver and Koosman.

But we did. As a matter of fact, the next day Aaron hit another homer, a three-run job, and the Braves knocked Koosman out with five runs in the fifth inning. Fortunately, we'd gone into the fifth with a 9–1 lead, most of it against our old friend Ron Reed.

We'd scored a gift run in the first on a crazy-hop grounder by Kranepool. In the second Koosman walked (the first tip-off that Reed could be had—Koosman can't even hit in batting practice) and Agee hit a home run to give us a 3–0 lead. I got a double, and Shamsky drove me home with a single, and that was all for Reed. But it didn't matter who Atlanta brought in to pitch.

We made it 6–0 off Paul Doyle in the third and 8–0 off Milt Pappas in the fourth. Still, when the Braves unloaded on Koosman, they came to within three runs, 9–6. That was the score when I came up in the seventh with Agee on third and two out. Tommie had singled, stolen second, and gone on to third on an infield out. All I could think of was getting him home. A lead of four runs would look a lot fatter than three.

The pitcher was Cecil Upshaw, a breaking-ball pitcher who'd never impressed me too much. I figured I could time one of his curves and take a pretty good cut. And there it was, a hanging curve. I timed, swung, and connected, and then I saw Agee —*a foot from my bat.* He was trying to steal home, and I'd almost knocked his head off on my follow-through. Tommie and I just sort of stood there and stared at each other as the ball curved foul. Maybe we even thanked God, the way you do when you're driving along and you just miss a serious accident. Neither of us could believe that I'd almost killed him.

The only time a man gets the sign to steal home is on a squeeze play, but with two out, there was no squeeze on. Tommie took a long lead off Upshaw and then realized that nobody in the park, including the nine men on the field, figured he was serious. So he just kept coming. He thought I'd seen him out of the corner of my eye and I'd back off. Tommie got a fantastic jump, and with the big curve coming in, he'd have scored standing up. But the big curve was all I saw until after I swung and hit the ball. Then I saw Agee. With the strangest expression on his face.

After a couple of seconds he walked back to third. I walked away from the batter's box and tried to get myself together. I kept telling myself, "Forget all that, there's a man on third and you've got to get him across." I looked for another curve. Two pitches later it came. The ball didn't hang as much as the first one had, so I didn't pull it foul. I hit it into the seats in straightaway left field, a two-run homer. Our lead was up to 11–6, and that's the way the game wound up.

Atlanta Airport on a Sunday night is like any other big-city airport. First we hit a traffic jam; then we couldn't locate the plane; then we waited forever for takeoff instructions. But after we took off, the pilot came on. "Gentlemen," he said, "congratulations. You were ahead of the Braves yesterday, you were ahead of them today, and you're ahead of them now. Their plane is still on the ground."

Everybody aboard laughed. Winners laugh at anything, even the pilot's bad jokes.

The third game of the play-offs was like the first two. Hank Aaron hit a home run, and we hit everything in sight. The Braves' pitcher was Pat Jarvis, another right-hander. Our lefty lineup—Agee, Garrett, Jones, Shamsky, Boswell, Kranepool, Grote, Harrelson—had belted two other righties, and we figured they were better than Jarvis.

We were right. From the first pitch, we were grooving on Jarvis. But we didn't score, because every ball seemed to go right at one of the Braves' fielders. We were backing them up to the ball or hitting screeching line drives that were turned into double plays. And Aaron's homer off Gary Gentry in the first inning had given the Braves a 2–0 lead.

In the third inning Gonzalez singled and Aaron doubled. Then Rico Carty hit a line drive off the left field wall, just foul. Hodges walked out of the dugout. I thought he might want to settle Gentry down a little. But Gil had seen enough. He had Nolan Ryan ready in the bullpen and decided to make a change right there, before the game could get out of hand. Ryan came in, struck out Carty and Clete Boyer, and got out of the inning on an easy fly to me in left.

The move made Gil look like a genius, and it was a smart move. Jarvis and Gentry were both being hit hard. Hodges could bring in a Ryan. The Braves' manager, Luman Harris, had no Ryan in his bullpen. His best relief pitcher in the pennant race had been Hoyt Wilhelm, and Wilhelm was ineligible for the play-offs because he'd been traded to Atlanta after September 1.

In the third inning we started hitting the ball where the Braves' outfielders couldn't possibly reach it, over fences. Agee put us on the scoreboard with a homer, and Boswell gave us a 3–2 lead with another homer in the fourth. In the Atlanta fifth we fell behind again when Ryan got a little impatient with Orlando Cepeda and tried to blow a fast ball by him. In the majors you don't beat a hitter on speed alone. Cepeda slammed it so hard and high over the center-field fence that all Agee could do was stand and watch it.

Ryan led off our fifth with a ground single, and after Agee lined out, Garrett hit a high fly ball that bounced off the façade under the stands in right field for a two-run homer. That put us ahead 5–4. I got Jarvis out of the game with a double, and Boswell singled me home to make it 6–4. We got another run in the sixth on a double and a couple of bunts. After that Ryan was untouchable. We won 7–4.

There was another mob scene on the field, but this time I'd made sure the bullpen gate would be left open. After the third out in the ninth, a grounder to third, I took off for the bullpen and made it around to the clubhouse in time for all the fun. Somebody yelled, "Bring on the Orioles!" They'd swept three straight from the Twins. We were going to start the World Series Saturday in Baltimore. Excited? Certainly I was excited. Isn't a guy always excited when he's about to see his first World Series game?

13

Best Foot Forward

The TV people had it all figured out. At least one of the league play-offs would go the full five games, ending on Wednesday. Then a day for travel, another for a workout, and the series could start on Saturday, October 11. The TV people liked that because it meant the first two World Series games would be on a weekend, and, with a pair of off days thrown in, if there were sixth and seventh games, they would be televised the following weekend.

But of course neither play-off went beyond three games. We had the whole week to wait, from Monday to Saturday, for our first World Series game. "I can wait another week," Eddie Yost told me in the clubhouse when we showed up for a workout Wednesday at Shea. "I've been waiting for this for twenty-five years."

Yost is a coach who came to the Mets from the Washington Senators with Rube Walker and Joe Pignatano when Hodges made the switch in 1968. He'd been an outstanding third baseman in the American League, mostly with the Senators. Eddie was a kid from Brooklyn who'd been signed off the NYU campus in 1944 and had then gone into the Army. When he got out, he played twelve straight seasons in Washington, and the Senators finished in the second division for twelve straight seasons. The closest Yost had ever come to a pennant in eighteen years as a player and seven as a coach was in his last season with the Los Angeles Angels in 1962. They finished third. But there are players like Eddie all over baseball, very good players who never get into a World Series. Just look at the Cubs—Ernie Banks, Ron Santo, Billy Williams, for instance—who've never made it. So I looked at a guy like Yost, and it got me to thinking how fine a spot we were in.

"You know," someone said in the clubhouse that afternoon, "whatever happens now, we've really shown them. We've proved something."

I forget who said it, but that doesn't matter. A lot of us were thinking it. And that was the wrong way to think when you were about to start a World Series. This was no time to cop out. "You read the papers and you think all Baltimore has to do is show up to win," I told Agee. "Everyone's telling us how good Baltimore is. But we'll be playing on grass on Saturday, not on paper. They're good ballplayers, but so are we or we wouldn't be here."

Sure, Baltimore had the name players, but the way we'd been playing, I felt that they weren't much better than we were. And as things turned out, they weren't even as good. The thing we had to do was play our regular game, remain aggressive, and capitalize on the kinds of things we had going for us all year. We weren't supposed to be in the World Series, and we weren't supposed to be in the play-offs, and we weren't supposed to be in the pennant race.

We never did get to work out Wednesday because it rained in New York. But we worked at Shea Thursday and then took off for Baltimore. We practiced at Memorial Stadium Friday. The outfield measurements weren't too different from Shea except down the foul lines, which were only 309 feet away from the plate compared to 340. Then they jutted out to 370 feet in straightaway left and right and curved out to 410 in center. But if the field was shaped something like Shea, it seemed a million miles away. Memorial Stadium was made of drab brick and concrete, a very colorless place. "Well," I thought, "we'll have a couple of days to liven it up."

I walked away from the home plate area, where the players and the reporters and the television crews were, out toward left field, where I'd be playing the next day. I tried to visualize what it would be like. I saw myself getting three or four hits and making great catches. Then I walked back in to take hitting practice.

I heard the voice when I was taking my cuts in the batting cage. I hadn't heard it since the All-Star Game in Washington in July, but I think I could identify that voice if I didn't hear it for fifty years. "Hey, Jones, you'd *better* take some practice. You'll need it for our pitchers!" It was Paul Blair, the man the Orioles call Motormouth. I could've told them that years before he ever wore a Baltimore uniform. I could've also told them something else they'd found out about Paul—that there isn't a more decent, hard-working guy going. We kidded back and forth and told each other how many hits we'd get, and finally one of us said, "Put your money where your mouth is." That was a joke. Blair probably didn't have that much money. Hell, there might not be *that* much money in circulation. But we settled on a friendly bet, ten dollars, on who'd get more hits in the Series.

After our workout Friday we had a team meeting to discuss the Orioles. We'd had scouts watching them at the end of the regular season and in the play-offs, and we went up and down the lineup discussing how each man would be pitched. And, at least in the report, each man had a weakness.

"Buford . . . Better hitter from the left side, bunts well, runs good, likes the ball pitched inside when he's batting left-handed. Hits the hard stuff. Not good on breaking stuff. . . .

"Blair . . . You can crowd him, and you can throw him breaking stuff away. Not a very good breaking ball hitter, especially weak on sliders away. . . .

"Frank Robinson . . . Likes the ball inside where he can jerk it. If you're going to pitch him in, pitch him bad in, way in. Otherwise stay outside. . . .

"Brooks Robinson . . . You can jam him. Give him good stuff and keep it on his fists. . . .

"Boog Powell . . . Move the ball around on him. Go in bad and then out over the plate for your strikes. No off-speed stuff at all unless it's very bad. He's a great off-speed hitter. Get him out on hard stuff away. . . .

"Hendricks . . . Good inside fast-ball hitter, good fast-ball hitter in general. Try to give him only breaking stuff if you can. Likes to pull the ball, so throw him in bad and make him pull it foul, then keep it away. . . .

"Belanger . . . Give him good stuff and jam him. He's had a fine season, but he's not that good a hitter if he's pitched to. . . .

"Johnson . . . Same thing. Jam him and give him good, hard stuff. Make him hit your best."

As we went over the hitters, I made mental notes. I figured on playing Frank Robinson and Elrod Hendricks to pull but Boog Powell straightaway. If we were pitching fast balls out over the plate to Powell, he didn't figure to pull. None of the others were pull hitters, so I'd start straightaway on all of them and take it from there.

This was all done at the team meeting, which was held after the pitchers and catchers had their own meeting. They went over each hitter in more detail, talking about specific types of pitches to throw in specific situations, going over every detail, any little thing our scouts might have seen that could wind up helping us to win a game.

Actually, though, the team meetings for the World Series weren't very different from those all season. We may have studied a little more because we weren't familiar with some of the players. But the procedure was the same. It was all the same. Three strikes and you were out, nine men on a side, and all that. They didn't change the rules for the Series. There was no reason to be nervous, and I know I *wasn't* nervous. The big crowds, the television, the reporters, we had had all that before. The $20,000? That was all the more reason to bear down and play your game.

One of the few Baltimore players we knew firsthand was their opening-game pitcher, Mike Cuellar, a tough left-hander who'd pitched for Houston until the Orioles got him for Curt Blefary, a catcher-first baseman, before the 1969 season. Cuellar had a 23–11 record in 1969 with a 2.38 earned-run average. Good numbers, but our guy was Tom Seaver, 25–7 and 2.21 ERA.

There was talk before the game that Gil might go with our left-handed lineup against Cuellar because of his screwball. It's thrown with the spin in the opposite direction of a curve, and it breaks the other way. Cuellar's screwball would break in to a lefty and out to a righty. But Gil went righty-lefty anyway, on the theory that a right-handed hitter could still see the motion more clearly, and the screwball wasn't Cuellar's only pitch. He had a good curve and a decent enough fast ball, plus the scroogie.

We knew Cuellar would be cool and tough. He was. They knew Seaver had the potential to be unbeatable. He wasn't. Don Buford, the Orioles' leadoff man, hit the second pitch of the game over the fence in right field to give Baltimore a 1–0 lead. After that Tom got outs, but just as he'd seemed to struggle in Atlanta the week before, again he didn't seem himself. In the fourth it caught up with him. Hendricks singled to right, Johnson walked, and Belanger singled in a run. Then Cuellar singled and Buford doubled and we were down, 4–0.

Tom pitched out of it against the meat of the Orioles' lineup, but the damage was done. Cuellar was too solid a pitcher and too smart to give up a 4–0 lead very easily. Still, we might've had him in the seventh. We loaded the bases with one out and scored a run on Weis' sacrifice fly. Gaspar came up to pinch-hit in the pitcher's spot and hit a little grounder down the third-base line. Against twenty-three major-league third basemen, the ball would probably have gone for a hit. Half of them might not even have thrown to first. But we knew about Brooks Robinson. His glove beats people. He charged the ball and fired, and the inning was over. Two innings later, so was the game.

Talk about turning points. I'd have to say ours came a few seconds after the final out. We came into the clubhouse relaxed. "There's no way Baltimore can beat us." "We're going to beat 'em." "They're just not that good." You heard it all over the clubhouse. Their power hitters hadn't touched us all day. We'd been beaten by very ordinary players in a very ordinary game. Maybe we'd have been down if they'd clobbered us or if we'd thrown the game away. But instead we were up and loose.

That night Angela and I went to dinner with some fellows who'd come up from Mobile for the Series. Most of my friends wouldn't arrive until the Series reached New York on Tuesday, but a couple had made it. I'd bought Series tickets for a number of people. For some—like Clyde Gray and his wife and Mrs. McCants and her brother—it was the least I could do. But when we made the Series, all sorts of people I barely knew called me up asking about tickets. I guess some of them didn't realize that in the Series players have to buy the tickets, because I was stiffed for quite a few. I bought tickets for people who never showed up to claim them and for others who never managed to write out a check for them. In the end, I was out something over $300.

There are always some people who take advantage of you or have no regard for you. They'll come up to you at a restaurant and stick a pen and a piece of paper under your nose for an autograph. They don't even wait, sometimes, for the fork to come out of your mouth. And at a sports dinner, they'll do anything they can to keep you around until all hours of the night. The real baseball fans are great, and I don't mind going out of my way for them. In New York the fans probably had as much to do with us winning the pennant as anything else. But there are always a few who forget you're a human being, too.

We broke away from our friends fairly early and went back to the hotel. I'd pretty much psyched myself into thinking that the Series was just another set of big games, but after all, it *was* the World Series, and I wanted as much rest as I could possibly get.

The next day at the ball park Blair got on me pretty good. "What happened to your four games?" he screeched at me. "I thought you guys were gonna beat us four straight."

I walked over and looked him straight in the eye. "I didn't say which four, did I?" I told him. "We're still gonna beat you four straight." Blair laughed and walked away. In the next few days the Orioles were about to find out how the other guys lived. When they started losing, they blamed it on everything but themselves or us. Frank Robinson and a few of the others said some things to the reporters that they shouldn't have. We'd heard it all before: They were good and we were lucky. Then, when they realized they could actually lose the Series, the Orioles tightened up completely. They were so busy talking they forgot to play. I really don't think they fully understood what was happening to them until they walked into the showers after the fifth game and the cold water hit them.

Dave McNally was Baltimore's second-game pitcher against Jerry Koosman. We'd been told McNally had a major-league fast ball that would rise up and in on you, a curve ball, and a slider. We knew he wasn't a bad pitcher. He had a 20–7 record.

We scored first, on a homer by Donn Clendenon in the fourth inning. Koosman was putting the ball where he wanted it, and we were making the plays behind him. Going into the seventh inning, Jerry had a no-hitter. Then in the seventh Blair singled, stole second, and scored on Brooks Robinson's single up the middle. Two hits and it was tied. The Baltimore fans were roaring, and some of the Orioles looked smug, as if they figured there was no way they could lose to us.

Both teams did nothing in the eighth, and I guess the Orioles felt pretty confident we'd fold, down one game already and caught from behind like that. But in the ninth, with two out, we scored the kind of run that had been winning games for us all year. Eddie Charles hit a ground single through the left side. That brought Grote up. With a 2–2 count, Hodges flashed the hit-and-run sign to Yost, our third-base coach, who passed it to Charles and Grote. Grote singled to left, and Charles, running on the pitch, made third base. That brought Al Weis up, and George Bamberger, Baltimore's pitching coach, walked out to the mound to confer with McNally. They were all looking into our dugout, waiting to see if Gil would hit for Weis. And Gil looked right back at them.

If any one New York Met was a product of Hodges' work, it was Al Weis. Gil changed Al from a switch-hitter to a right-handed hitter; he worked on Al's stance; he had Al swinging different style bats, sometimes heavier, sometimes lighter. You don't turn your back on a man because it's the World Series. If you undercut your players like that, you wouldn't be in the Series in the first place. McNally hung a slider, and Weis ripped it, a solid single to left. Charles trotted home, and we were ahead 2–1.

McNally got Koosman for the third out, and we went to the bottom of the ninth. Jerry looked tired, but all we needed were three outs, then two, then one. Frank Robinson was up with none on and two down. Hodges sent Weis, the second baseman, into left field and swung us around so that we had four out-fielders. It was the same shift he'd used against Richie Allen and Willie McCovey, daring Robinson to give up his shot at a long ball for an almost certain single. Frank played it straight and drew a walk. Then Powell walked, and Hodges brought Ron Taylor in to pitch to Brooks Robinson. Merv Rettenmund, who'd run for Frank, was on second, a hit away from tying the game again.

The count to Brooks went 3–2, and then he hit one to third, on the ground. I raced in, just in case, and breathed a little easier when I saw Charles had picked the ball up. But suddenly I saw something terrible happening right in front of me. Charles started for third, where he just had to tag the bag for a force out. But the ball wasn't hit too hard, and Rettenmund had a good start off second. With a decent slide he would beat Eddie to the base. I moaned, "No . . . ," but just as I did, Eddie straightened up and, cool as he could be, fired across to Clendenon to get Brooks by a couple of steps. We won. "You old man, you beau-tiful old man," I thought all the way into the dugout, down the ramp, and into the clubhouse.

We had the next day off—travel time back to New York—and went into the third game at Shea Tuesday. After Ryan's big relief job against Atlanta in the play-offs, there was some talk that Hodges might go with Nolan instead of Gary Gentry in the third game of the Series. But we knew he wouldn't. Gil doesn't operate that way. Gentry had won thirteen games for us in this rookie season. He had a lot to learn, but he'd learned a lot. Besides, Ryan was used to the bullpen, and Gentry wasn't. If you started Ryan, that meant you had one less big arm available in relief. Baltimore's starter was Jim Palmer, who supposedly had the best arm of anyone on the Orioles' staff. That was going to be their big edge, having Palmer, with his 16–4 record, ready for the third game. We had our edge, too, the 55,000 friendly faces (even Jackie Kennedy was there) ready to tear the place apart if we won.

Gentry got the Orioles out in the first, and in the bottom half

Agee worked Palmer to a 2–1 count. You don't want to walk the leadoff hitter. Then again, as things turned out, Palmer would've settled for a walk. He came in too fat with the 2–1 pitch, and Agee hit it back at him—about 420 feet back. The ball carried over the center-field wall, and we were ahead 1–0.

In the second, we got two men on with one out and Gentry up. The Oriole outfielders came in very shallow, protecting against an accidental single. You do that when you've got a hard thrower like Palmer out there, and usually it pays off. The bloopers are caught. But once in a while the fly balls aren't. Gentry hit it over everyone's head in right center, two runs scored, and we had a 3–0 lead.

Then in the fourth the Orioles got something going. But it only set up the first half of the greatest two-act show an outfielder has ever put on in the World Series. If we all live to be a hundred years old, we may not see anything like it again.

With men on first and third and two out, Hendricks tagged one to deep left center. I took off after the ball, but I had no chance. Agee, who had been playing a deep center, but around to right, had the only shot at the ball, and it was heading away from him. Tommie took one last huge stride, jumped at the ball, and hit the fence. I was only a few feet away, and I was ready for the ball to bounce away. But it was safely in Tommie's glove. We were out of the inning.

And that was only half of it. We scored another run in the sixth and led, 4–0, into the seventh. With two out, Gentry walked three straight hitters, and Gil called in Ryan to pitch to Paul Blair. Nolan got two quick strikes on Blair, and with the bases loaded he wasn't about to fool around. But Paul was playing for the same twenty grand. He hit a shot to deep right-center. Agee was off with the crack of the bat, and he never stopped going. Like Hendricks' smash in the fourth, Blair's was hit to the opposite field, and it was tailing away from Tommie. At the last instant Tommie dove for it. He came down hard on the dirt track in front of the fence, the ball in his glove.

For a second I think you could've heard a pin drop on second base. Everyone was prepared for a triple, maybe even an inside-the-park homer the way Blair can run. And then there was

Tommie, making the play. After that first second, the roar was tremendous. I don't think I've ever heard as loud an ovation for anyone in my life, and I doubt that I ever will. I remembered the first time Tommie had gotten a standing ovation at Shea, in April, 1968, when he got his first hit in thirty-five at-bats. Don't think he didn't remember it, either. You come up the way Tommie and I did, and you don't have to play like you're humble. It comes naturally.

Kranepool put us ahead 5–0 with a homer in the eighth. The Orioles loaded the bases with two out in the ninth, but this time Ryan didn't need any help in the outfield. He struck out Blair to end the game. We were up two games to one. There were so many fans waiting for us that it took me a half hour to get from the players' exit to my car. But a half hour wasn't much. The fans had waited an hour and a half just to pat us on the back and get our autographs.

In the clubhouse before the fourth game I walked by Agee's locker. "Thanks," I said.

He looked up. "For what?"

"You held me even with my man, that's what." And we both laughed. The composite box score the newspapers print after each game showed my totals and Blair's were the same. We were each one for twelve after three games.

You can't really say you're in a slump based on the three games. I'd hit a couple of line drives that were caught. But except for the joking that went with my friendly bet with Blair, my totals weren't bothering me. The idea in October wasn't any different than it had been in April. The idea was to win games. And we had just two more to win, with Seaver and Koosman going for us.

Clendenon gave Seaver a 1–0 lead in the second inning of the fourth game with a homer off Cuellar, and for a long time it looked like that was all Tom would need. He was on his game when he had to be and still had a shutout in the ninth. He seemed to be breezing by then. But with one out, Frank Robinson and Boog Powell singled, bringing Brooks Robinson up. Frank had reached third on Boog's hit, so a fly ball would tie the score. Robinson hit a line drive to short right center, and

Swoboda made a play that may have been better than each of Agee's were, individually. He raced in and toward center, dove, and caught the ball, tumbling forward. Frank Robinson scored after the catch to tie the game, but Ron had saved it.

Seaver pitched out of trouble in the tenth, and Grote led off our half with a fly to short left. Buford started back, then came on, but it was too late. Belanger, the shortstop, took a dive at it and missed. Grote had a double. Gaspar went in to run for Grote, and the Orioles walked Weis to set up a force play with Seaver due up.

Gil sent J. C. Martin up to hit for Tom. Dick Hall, a right-hander, had started the inning for Baltimore (they had pinch-hit for Cuellar in the eighth), but the Orioles went for Pete Richert to pitch to Martin. Gil stayed with J. C., because all he wanted was a sacrifice bunt. We knew that, the Orioles knew that, and I guess the 50,000 fans knew it, too. Martin laid down the most beautiful sacrifice bunt I've ever seen. It rolled about twelve feet away, between the mound and the first base line, and died. Richert reached the ball pretty quickly, but it was so well placed Martin might have beaten it out. We'll never know. Richert's throw hit on the wrist and rolled away; Gaspar came around third and scored the winning run. The way we jumped up and down and hugged each other, you'd have thought that we'd just won the World Series. But we hadn't. We had one more game to win.

That night Angela and I took all of our friends from out of town to dinner at Concertine's Restaurant on Hillside Avenue—we had about a dozen people up for the Series by then, and it was getting a little hard to walk in the door of our apartment.

I got a kick out of seeing all of them there. Some were guys from Mobile who hadn't been particularly close to me down there, and I guess for them watching me play was a kind of fulfillment. We'd all been ballplayers in Plateau, and we'd all had dreams. And now a couple of us were living the dreams, and these other fellows just had to be there to see it. Then there were the very special people. My cousin, James Davis, came down from Buffalo. James had helped Angela and me through a few rough spots when I played up there in the International League.

And Mrs. McCants. She knew and I knew that without her there was no way I'd have been playing major-league baseball. And Clyde Gray, the guy who wrote the letter to Casey Stengel and drove me to Atlanta so I could try out for the Mets. Clyde sat next to me at dinner and gave me his impressions of all the players and tried to tell me why he thought I wasn't hitting the ball too well in the Series.

I'd gotten another hit in the fourth game, my second of the Series, but now I wasn't thinking about that at all. We were only one game away from the world championship. And there was no way we could lose. The Series was going like the season had. Our pitching was great, and our hitting and fielding were there when we needed them. One more. All we needed was one more.

It didn't come easy. In the third inning of the fifth game McNally hit a two-run homer, and Frank Robinson hit one, too, and we were down, 3–0. But Koosman hung on after that and regained his rhythm. I got the feeling, watching him work from left field, that the Orioles weren't going to do any more scoring. All we had to do was find three runs.

We found the first two on my shoe. I led off the sixth against McNally. He'd been giving me off-speed stuff mostly, and one of his curves broke way in and ticked off the inside of my right foot. Then it bounced into the dirt and rolled into the Met dugout. I started for first base, but Lou DiMuro, the home plate ump, called me back. He said the ball had simply hit the dirt, not me. I said, "My foot, it did," or something like that. Then we both looked at Hodges, who was walking out of our dugout with the ball. Gil showed the ball to DiMuro and pointed to a blur of shoe polish, which had rubbed off when the ball hit my foot. DiMuro waved me to first base. I told Powell when I got there, "I wonder if Blair will let that count?" We were still tied with two hits apiece.

But I didn't stick around first very long. Clendenon, the next batter, hit his third homer of the Series, and my slightly scuffed shoe was trotting around the bases in front of him. We tied it at 3–3 in the seventh on a homer by Al Weis, and it was still 3–3 when I led off the eighth.

I walked out with Clendenon, who was going to the on-deck circle. "No sweat," I told him. "Look how much I got done with my foot last time. Think what I'd do if I ever used my bat."

The Orioles had hit for McNally in the eighth, and their new pitcher was Eddie Watt, an off-speed relief pitcher. I decided to take a look at what he had, and he threw me three straight balls. Then he grooved a strike. "If I see another one like that," I thought, "then I'm through shopping around." I hit the next pitch over Blair's head and off the center-field wall for a double. Gil passed the bunt sign on to Clendenon, but Donn bunted foul twice, sliced a high drive foul down the right-field line, and then grounded out. I was still on second, with one out. Swoboda pulled a liner to deep left, and I figured we had them. Buford almost caught up with it. I waited, watched the ball go by him, and scooted around third and in to score the run that won the World Series. Swoboda scored another run a few seconds later when Powell and Watt both made errors on Grote's smash to first.

Then Koosman went out and pitched the ninth inning.

And with two out and Frank Robinson at first, Dave Johnson hit *that* fly ball to me in left.

"Come on down, baby. Come on down."

Appendix: Records

CLEON JOSEPH JONES

Born August 4, 1942, at Plateau, Alabama

Height: 6-0. Weight: 195. Throws: Left. Bats: Right.

Year	Team	(Class)	Pos	G	AB	R	H	2B	3B	HR	RBI	SB	BA
1963	Auburn	(A)	OF	14	50	19	18	1	3	1	6	4	.360
1963	Raleigh	(A)	OF	49	177	28	54	5	6	2	23	20	.305
1963	Mets	(NL)	OF	6	15	1	2	0	0	0	1	0	.133
1964	Buffalo	(AAA)	OF	137	500	96	139	22	6	16	70	12	.278
1965	Buffalo	(AAA)	OF	123	454	61	122	15	3	15	49	14	.269
1965	Mets	(NL)	OF	30	74	2	11	1	0	1	9	1	.149
1966	Mets	(NL)	OF	139	495	74	136	16	4	8	57	16	.275
1967	Mets	(NL)	OF	129	411	46	101	10	5	5	30	12	.246
1968	Mets	(NL)	OF	147	509	63	151	29	4	14	55	23	.297
1969	Mets	(NL)	OF-1B	137	483	92	164	25	4	12	75	16	.340
Major League Totals				588	1987	278	565	81	17	40	227	70	.284

PLAY OFF RECORD

Year	Team	(Class)	Pos	G	AB	R	H	2B	3B	HR	RBI	SB	BA
1969	Mets	(NL)	OF	3	14	4	6	2	0	1	4	2	.429

WORLD SERIES RECORD

Year	Team	(Class)	Pos	G	AB	R	H	2B	3B	HR	RBI	SB	BA
1969	Mets	(NL)	OF	5	19	2	3	1	0	0	0	0	.158

179

MET TEAM STANDINGS — 1962-1969

1962

Giants	103	62	.624
Dodgers	102	63	.618
Reds.	98	64	.605
Pirates	93	68	.578
Braves	86	76	.531
Cardinals	84	78	.519
Phillies	81	80	.503
Astros	64	96	.400
Cubs	59	103	.364
METS	40	120	.250

1963

Dodgers	99	63	.611
Cardinals	93	69	.574
Giants	88	74	.543
Phillies	87	75	.537
Reds	86	76	.531
Braves	84	78	.519
Cubs	82	80	.506
Pirates	74	88	.457
Astros	66	96	.407
METS	51	111	.315

1964

Cardinals	93	69	.574
Phillies	92	70	.568
Reds	92	70	.568
Giants	90	72	.556
Braves	88	74	.543
Dodgers	80	82	.494
Pirates	80	82	.494
Cubs	76	86	.469
Astros	66	96	.407
METS	53	109	.327

1965

Dodgers	97	65	.599
Giants	95	67	.586
Pirates	90	72	.556
Reds	89	73.	.549
Braves	86	76	.531
Phillies	85	76	.528
Cardinals	80	81	.497
Cubs	72	90	.444
Astros	65	97	.401
METS	50	112	.309

1966

Dodgers	95	67	.586
Giants	93	68	.578
Pirates	92	70	.568
Phillies	87	75	.537
Braves	85	77	.525
Cardinals	83	79	.512
Reds	76	84	.475
Astros	72	90	.444
METS	66	95	.410
Cubs	59	103	.364

1967

Cardinals	101	60	.627
Giants	91	71	.562
Cubs	87	74	.540
Reds	87	75	.537
Phillies	82	80	.506
Pirates	81	81	.500
Braves	77	85	.475
Dodgers	73	89	.451
Astros	69	93	.426
METS	61	101	.377

MET TEAM STANDINGS – 1962–1969 (Continued)

1968

Cardinals	97	65	.599
Giants	88	74	.543
Cubs	84	78	.519
Reds	83	79	.512
Braves	81	80	.500
Pirates	80	82	.494
Phillies	76	86	.469
Dodgers	76	86	.469
METS	73	89	.451
Astros	72	90	.444

1969

EASTERN DIVISION				WESTERN DIVISION			
*METS	100	62	.617	Braves	93	69	.574
Cubs	92	70	.568	Giants	90	72	.568
Pirates	88	74	.549	Reds	89	73	.549
Cardinals	87	75	.537	Dodgers	85	77	.525
Phillies	63	99	.389	Astros	81	81	.500
Expos	52	110	.321	Padres	52	110	.321

*Mets won play-off, 3 games to 0.

NATIONAL LEAGUE'S LEADING HITTERS

1968

PLAYER, TEAM	GAMES	AT-BATS	RUNS	HITS	AVERAGE
Pete Rose, Reds	149	626	94	210	.335
Matty Alou, Pirates	146	558	59	185	.332
Felipe Alou, Braves	160	662	72	210	.317
Alex Johnson, Reds	149	603	79	188	.312
Curt Flood, Cardinals	150	618	71	186	.301
CLEON JONES, METS	147	509	63	151	.297
Glenn Beckert, Cubs	155	643	98	189	.294
Willie McCovey, Giants	148	523	81	153	.293
Rusty Staub, Astros	161	591	54	172	.291
Roberto Clemente, Pirates	132	502	74	146	.291

1969

PLAYER, TEAM	GAMES	AT-BATS	RUNS	HITS	AVERAGE
Pete Rose, Reds	156	627	120	216	.348
Roberto Clemente, Pirates	138	507	87	175	.345
CLEON JONES, METS	137	483	92	164	.340
Matty Alou, Pirates	162	698	105	231	.331
Willie McCovey, Giants	149	491	101	157	.320
Alex Johnson, Reds	139	523	86	165	.315
Willie Davis, Dodgers	129	498	66	155	.311
Willie Stargell, Pirates	145	522	89	160	.307
Bobby Tolan, Reds	152	637	104	195	.306
Manny Sanguillen, Pirates	129	459	62	139	.303

METS' 1969 GAME-BY-GAME MARCH
TO THE WORLD CHAMPIONSHIP

Date	Opponent	Score	Winning Pitcher	Losing Pitcher	Record	Pos.	Games Behind
4/8	Montreal	10-11	Shaw	Koonce	0-1	4th	1
4/9	Montreal	9-5	McGraw	Stoneman	1-1	3rd	1
4/10	Montreal	4-2	Gentry	Jaster	2-1	3rd	1
4/11	St. Louis	5-6	Carlton	Koosman	2-2	3rd	2
4/12	St. Louis	0-1	Giusti	Cardwell	2-3	3rd	2
4/13	St. Louis	1-3	Gibson	Seaver	2-4	5th	3½
4/14	at Philadelphia	1-5	Fryman	McAndrew	2-5	5th	4
4/15	at Philadelphia	6-3	Gentry	Wagner	3-5	4th	4
4/16	at Pittsburgh	3-11	Moose	Koosman	3-6	5th	4
4/17	at Pittsburgh	0-4	Bunning	Cardwell	3-7	5th	5
4/19	at St. Louis	2-1	Seaver	Gibson	4-7	4th	6
4/20	at St. Louis	11-3	Ryan	Briles	5-7	3rd	5½
4/21	Philadelphia	1-2	Fryman	Taylor	5-8	3rd	6
4/23	Pittsburgh	2-0	Koosman	Bunning	6-8	3rd	4½
4/25	Chicago	1-3	Jenkins	Seaver	6-9	4th	5
4/26	Chicago	3-9	Hands	Cardwell	6-10	5th	6
4/27	Chicago	6-8	Regan	Koonce	6-11		
	Chicago	3-0	McGraw	Nye	7-11	4th	6
4/29	at Montreal	2-0	Ryan	Grant	8-11	3rd	6½
4/30	at Montreal	2-1	Seaver	Wegener	9-11	3rd	6
5/1	at Montreal	2-3	Face	Cardwell	9-12	4th	6
5/2	at Chicago	4-6	Holtzman	Gentry	9-13	5th	7
5/3	at Chicago	2-3	Regan	Koonce	9-14	5th	8
5/4	at Chicago	3-2	Seaver	Hands	10-14		
	at Chicago	3-2	McGraw	Selma	11-14	4th	6
5/6	Cincinnati	8-1	Cardwell	Nolan	12-14	4th	6
5/7	Cincinnati	0-3	Merritt	Gentry	12-15	4th	6
5/10	Houston	3-1	Seaver	Lemaster	13-15	3rd	5
5/11	Houston	1-4	Dierker	Cardwell	13-16		
	Houston	11-7	Koonce	Wilson	14-16	3rd	6
5/13	Atlanta	3-4	Reed	Gentry	14-17	3rd	7
5/14	Atlanta	9-3	Seaver	Niekro	15-17	3rd	7
5/15	Atlanta	5-6	Jarvis	Cardwell	15-18	3rd	7½

Date	Opponent	Score	Winning Pitcher	Losing Pitcher	Record	Pos.	Games Behind
5/16	at Cincinnati	10-9	Koonce	Culver	16-18	3rd	7½
5/17	at Cincinnati	11-3	Gentry	Maloney	17-18	3rd	6½
5/21	at Atlanta	5-0	Seaver	Niekro	18-18	2nd	5½
5/22	at Atlanta	3-15	Jarvis	McGraw	18-19	3rd	6½
5/23	at Houston	0-7	Griffin	Gentry	18-20	4th	7½
5/24	at Houston	1-5	Dierker	Koosman	18-21	4th	8½
5/25	at Houston	3-6	Lemaster	Seaver	18-22	4th	9
5/27	San Diego	2-3	Santorini	McAndrew	18-23	4th	9
5/28	San Diego	1-0 (11)	McGraw	McCool	19-23	4th	9
5/30	San Francisco	4-3	Seaver	Linzy	20-23	4th	9
5/31	San Francisco	4-2	Gentry	Perry	21-23	3rd	9
6/1	San Francisco	5-4	Taylor	Gibbon	22-23	3rd	9
6/2	Los Angeles	2-1	Koosman	Osteen	23-23	3rd	8½
6/3	Los Angeles	5-2	Seaver	Foster	24-23	2nd	8½
6/4	Los Angeles	1-0 (14)	Taylor	Mikkelsen	25-23	2nd	8½
6/6	at San Diego	5-3	Gentry	Ross	26-23	2nd	8½
6/7	at San Diego	4-1	Koosman	Podres	27-23	2nd	8
6/8	at San Diego	3-2	Seaver	Santorini	28-23	2nd	7½
6/10	at San Francisco	9-4	Cardwell	McCormick	29-23	2nd	6½
6/11	at San Francisco	2-7	Perry	Gentry	29-24	2nd	7
6/13	at Los Angeles	0-1	Foster	Koosman	29-25	2nd	8
6/14	at Los Angeles	3-1	Seaver	Sutton	30-25	2nd	8
6/15	at Los Angeles	2-3	Drysdale	DiLauro	30-26	2nd	8½
6/17	at Philadelphia	1-0	Gentry	Champion	31-26		
	at Philadelphia	3-7	Jackson	Cardwell	31-27	2nd	6
6/18	at Philadelphia	2-0	Koosman	Wise	32-27	2nd	6
6/19	at Philadelphia	6-5	Taylor	Raffo	33-27	2nd	5½
6/20	St. Louis	4-3	Ryan	Gibson	34-27	2nd	5½
6/21	St. Louis	3-5	Briles	DiLauro	34-28	2nd	5½
6/22	St. Louis	5-1	Gentry	Carlton	35-28		
	St. Louis	1-0	Koosman	Torrez	36-28	2nd	4½
6/24	Philadelphia	2-1	Seaver	Fryman	37-28		
	Philadelphia	5-0	McAndrew	Johnson	38-28	2nd	4½

Date	Opponent	Score	Winning Pitcher	Losing Pitcher	Record	Pos.	Games Behind
6/25	Philadelphia	5-6 (10)	Wilson	Taylor	38-29	2nd	5½
6/26	Philadelphia	0-2	Jackson	Cardwell	38-30	2nd	6
6/27	Pittsburgh	1-3	Blass	Koosman	38-31	2nd	7
6/28	Pittsburgh	4-7	Bunning	Gentry	38-32	2nd	8
6/29	Pittsburgh	7-3	Seaver	Veale	39-32	2nd	8
6/30	at St. Louis	10-2	McAndrew	Briles	40-32	2nd	6
7/1	at St. Louis	1-4	Carlton	Ryan	40-33		
	at St. Louis	5-8	Torrez	DiLauro	40-34	2nd	7½
7/2	at St. Louis	6-4 (14)	McGraw	Willis	41-34	2nd	7½
7/3	at St. Louis	8-1	Gentry	Grant	42-34	2nd	7½
7/4	at Pittsburgh	11-6	Seaver	Veale	43-34		
	at Pittsburgh	9-2	Cardwell	Ellis	44-34	2nd	7
7/6	at Pittsburgh	8-7	Taylor	Hartenstein	45-34	2nd	5
7/8	Chicago	4-3	Koosman	Jenkins	46-34	2nd	4
7/9	Chicago	4-0	Seaver	Holtzman	47-34	2nd	3
7/10	Chicago	2-6	Hands	Gentry	47-35	2nd	4
7/11	Montreal	4-11	Wegener	McAndrew	47-36	2nd	4
7/13	Montreal	4-3	Koosman	Robertson	48-36		
	Montreal	9-7	Koonce	McGinn	49-36	2nd	4½
7/14	at Chicago	0-1	Hands	Seaver	49-37	2nd	5½
7/15	at Chicago	5-4	Gentry	Selma	50-37	2nd	4½
7/16	at Chicago	9-5	Koonce	Jenkins	51-37	2nd	3½
7/18	at Montreal	5-2	Koosman ·	Robertson	52-37	2nd	3½
7/19	at Montreal	4-5	Stoneman	Seaver	52-38	2nd	3½
7/20	at Montreal	2-3	Waslewski	Gentry	52-39		
	at Montreal	4-3 (10)	DiLauro	Face	53-39	2nd	4½
7/24	Cincinnati	3-4 (12)	Ramos	McGraw	53-40	2nd	5½
7/25	Cincinnati	4-3	Taylor	Carroll	54-40	2nd	4½
7/26	Cincinnati	3-2	Seaver	Cloninger	55-40	2nd	4½
7/27	Cincinnati	3-6	Arrigo	Cardwell	55-41	2nd	4½
7/30	Houston	3-16	Wilson	Koosman	55-42		
	Houston	5-11	Dierker	Gentry	55-43	2nd	5
7/31	Houston	0-2	Griffin	Seaver	55-44	2nd	6

METS' 1969 GAME-BY-GAME MARCH
TO THE WORLD CHAMPIONSHIP *(Continued)*

Date	Opponent	Score	Winning Pitcher	Losing Pitcher	Record	Pos.	Games Behind
8/1	Atlanta	5-4	Koonce	Niekro	56-44	2nd	6
8/2	Atlanta	1-0	McAndrew	Reed	57-44	2nd	6
8/3	Atlanta	6-5 (11)	Taylor	Raymond	58-44	2nd	6
8/4	at Cincinnati	0-1	Maloney	Koosman	58-45	2nd	7
8/5	at Cincinnati	5-8	Nolan	Seaver	58-46		
	at Cincinnati	10-1	Ryan	Arrigo	59-46	2nd	7½
8/6	at Cincinnati	2-3	Merritt	McAndrew	59-47	2nd	8½
8/8	at Atlanta	4-1	Koosman	Pappas	60-47		
	at Atlanta	0-1 (10)	Reed	Taylor	60-48	2nd	8
8/9	at Atlanta	5-3	Seaver	Stone	61-48	2nd	8
8/10	at Atlanta	3-0	Cardwell	Britton	62-48	2nd	7
8/11	at Houston	0-3	Griffin	McAndrew	62-49	2nd	7½
8/12	at Houston	7-8	Wilson	Koosman	62-50	2nd	8½
8/13	at Houston	2-8	Dierker	Gentry	62-51	3rd	9½
8/16	San Diego	2-0	Seaver	Sisk	63-51		
	San Diego	2-1	McAndrew	Ross	64-51	3rd	8½
8/17	San Diego	3-2	Koosman	Niekro	65-51		
	San Diego	3-2	Cardwell	Kirby	66-51	2nd	7½
8/19	San Francisco	1-0 (14)	McGraw	Marichal	67-51	2nd	7½
8/20	San Francisco	6-0	McAndrew	Perry	68-51	2nd	6½
8/21	San Francisco	6-7 (11)	McMahon	Taylor	68-52	2nd	6½
8/22	Los Angeles	5-3	Koosman	Singer	69-52	2nd	5½
8/23	Los Angeles	3-2	Taylor	Brewer	70-52	2nd	5½
8/24	Los Angeles	7-4	Koonce	Sutton	71-52	2nd	5½
8/26	at San Diego	8-4	Seaver	Sisk	72-52		
	at San Diego	3-0	McAndrew	Niekro	73-52	2nd	3
8/27	at San Diego	4-1	Koosman	Kirby	74-52	2nd	2
8/29	at San Francisco	0-5	Marichal	Gentry	74-53	2nd	3½
8/30	at San Francisco	3-2 (10)	McGraw	Perry	75-53	2nd	3½
8/31	at San Francisco	8-0	Seaver	McCormick	76-53		
	at San Francisco	2-3 (10)	Linzy	McGraw	76-54	2nd	4
9/1	at Los Angeles	6-10	Bunning	Koosman	76-55	2nd	4½
9/2	at Los Angeles	5-4	Gentry	Sutton	77-55	2nd	5

Date	Opponent	Score	Winning Pitcher	Losing Pitcher	Record	Pos.	Games Behind
9/3	at Los Angeles	4-5	Mikkelsen	DiLauro	77-56	2nd	5
9/5	Philadelphia	5-1	Seaver	Jackson	78-56		
	Philadelphia	2-4	Wise	McAndrew	78-57	2nd	4½
9/6	Philadelphia	3-0	Cardwell	Johnson	79-57	2nd	3½
9/7	Philadelphia	9-3	Ryan	Champion	80-57	2nd	2½
9/8	Chicago	3-2	Koosman	Hands	81-57	2nd	1½
9/9	Chicago	7-1	Seaver	Jenkins	82-57	2nd	½
9/10	Montreal	3-2 (12)	Taylor	Stoneman	83-57		
	Montreal	7-1	Ryan	Reed	84-57	1st	+1
9/11	Montreal	4-0	Gentry	Robertson	85-57	1st	+1½
9/12	at Pittsburgh	1-0	Koosman	Moose	86-57		
	at Pittsburgh	1-0	Cardwell	Ellis	87-57	1st	+2½
9/13	at Pittsburgh	5-2	Seaver	Walker	88-57	1st	+3½
9/14	at Pittsburgh	3-5	Blass	Ryan	88-58	1st	+3½
9/15	at St. Louis	4-3	McGraw	Carlton	89-58	1st	+4½
9/17	at Montreal	5-0	Koosman	Waslewski	90-58	1st	+4
9/18	at Montreal	2-0	Seaver	Stoneman	91-58	1st	+5
9/19	Pittsburgh	2-8	Veale	Ryan	91-59		
	Pittsburgh	0-8	Walker	McAndrew	91-60	1st	+4
9/20	Pittsburgh	0-4	Moose	Gentry	91-61	1st	+4
9/21	Pittsburgh	5-3	Koosman	Ellis	92-61		
	Pittsburgh	6-1	Cardwell	Blass	93-61	1st	+4½
9/22	St. Louis	3-1	Seaver	Briles	94-61	1st	+5½
9/23	St. Louis	3-2 (11)	McGraw	Gibson	95-61	1st	+5½
9/24	St. Louis	6-0	Gentry	Carlton	96-61	1st	+5½
9/26	at Philadelphia	5-0	Koosman	Fryman	97-61	1st	+6½
9/27	at Philadelphia	1-0	Seaver	Jackson	98-61	1st	+7½
9/28	at Philadelphia	2-0	Gentry	Johnson	99-61	1st	+8
10/1	at Chicago	6-5 (10)	Taylor	Selma	100-61	1st	+9
10/2	at Chicago	3-5	Decker	Cardwell	100-62	1st	+8
10/4	at Atlanta	9-5	Seaver	Niekro	1-0		
10/5	at Atlanta	11-6	Taylor	Reed	2-0		
10/6	Atlanta	7-4	Ryan	Jarvis	3-0		

METS' 1969 GAME-BY-GAME MARCH
TO THE WORLD CHAMPIONSHIP *(Continued)*

Date	Opponent	Score	Winning Pitcher	Losing Pitcher	Record	Pos.	Games Behind
10/11	at Baltimore	1-4	Cuellar	Seaver	0-1		
10/12	at Baltimore	2-1	Koosman	McNally	1-1		
10/14	Baltimore	5-0	Gentry	Palmer	2-1		
10/15	Baltimore	2-1 (10)	Seaver	Hall	3-1		
10/16	Baltimore	5-3	Koosman	Watt	4-1		

Cleon's Special Soul Food Dinner

by *Angela Jones*

The way the schedule breaks, with all the night games and road trips, Cleon and I don't get too much of a chance to entertain in New York But when we do have people over for dinner, Cleon is very partial to a few dishes that he has enjoyed all his life. Here's a typical menu.

Potato Salad
Candied Yams
Hamhocks and Greens
Hamhocks and Butterbeans
Corn Bread
Banana Pudding
Iced Tea

Recipe for Hamhocks and Greens/
Hamhocks and Butterbeans

Eight smoked hamhocks
Package of lima beans
Fresh collard greens
Sugar
Salt
Pepper
Whole garlic
Small onion
Vinegar

Boil six of the hamhocks in a three-quart saucepan for two hours, adding water if necessary. Add the lima beans, four to six sections of a clove of garlic, half a diced onion, and sugar, salt, and pepper to taste. Reduce flame and simmer for two more hours. Serve hot.

Boil the other two hamhocks in a smaller saucepan for three hours. Roll up the greens, slice them into bite-size portions, and add them to the hamhocks with sugar, salt, a dash of pepper, a touch of vinegar, and a few bits of the onion. Reduce flame until there is just enough heat to keep hamhocks and greens warm until serving.

Recipe for Corn Bread

One cup plain yellow corn meal
One-half cup flour
One tablespoon sugar
One teaspoon baking powder
A pinch of salt
One-half cup whole milk
One tablespoon lard

Mix everything but the lard together in a bowl, adding one-quarter cup of water if mixture gets too dry. Heat oven to 450 degrees. Put lard in an eight-inch bread pan and heat in the oven until the lard melts. Pour the excess lard into the bowl, mixing it in, and then pour the whole mixture back into the pan and heat for 15 to 20 minutes, or until bread rises in the center. It can be tested with a toothpick to see if the center is dry. Then place the bread under the oven's broiler for a few seconds until it browns. Slice and serve.

Recipe for Banana Pudding

One cup evaporated milk
One tablespoon flour
One cup sugar
Three eggs
Two tablespoons butter

One teaspoon lemon or vanilla extract
Bananas
Vanilla wafers

Mix milk, flour, and sugar and heat over lowest possible flame, being careful not to burn sugar. Whip the eggs, and after five minutes add them to the pan and turn off flame. Add the butter and extract. Cover the bottom and sides of a baking pan with wafers, add a layer of banana slices, a second layer of wafers, a second layer of banana slices, and a third layer of wafers. Pour the warm mixture into the pan and serve warm.

For a variation, you can make banana meringue pudding. Separate the whites from the yolks of the eggs, add sugar, and beat them to a high whip; then place the whites over the pudding and bake until the topping browns. Both the puddings can be chilled, but Cleon likes them warm, and I've found that if they are refrigerated, the wafers can get soggy and lose their soul.